PETER

FINDS

LIFE

DARYL T SANDERS

This book is a result of a personal Bible study where I reviewed every use of the name of Peter in the Gospels. I combined them when the use was a repeat and then described the revelation that Jesus was bringing in the context or what Peter was learning from it.

We will find in this book that Jesus was getting the leadership trained that would lead the church as it began in the Book of Acts. We can learn how Jesus prepares all of us for the plans and purposes He has for our lives.

You may contact me at 12dsanders@gmail.com for speaking engagements or questions or discussion about the material.

Other books by Daryl T Sanders are:
Peter Finds Power (Peter in the book of Acts)
Peter Finds Purpose (Peter in the epistles)
God the Father
wH**Y** – **Questions along life's journey**
Finding the Power to Heal
David, Chosen by God

All Bible references used the King James as found on the web site www.blueletterbible.org. Definitions are from Strong's Concordance.

CHAPTER ONE
THE CALL OF PETER:

Peter was one of the more controversial members of the inner circle of Jesus Christ. I probably have heard more sermons including the name Peter than any other of the disciples except perhaps the Apostle Paul. He is often castigated for his tendency to jump into the center of things at the "drop of a hat." Perhaps this is one of the reasons why he endeared himself to Jesus because he was willing to leap before he looked.

The truth of the matter is that Peter was one of three in the inner circle of the disciples. He was designated to be in more accounts of the miraculous with Jesus than any of the other disciples. This indicates that he was a man of faith – for Jesus only allowed men of faith to be with Him when He did the miraculous like raise the dead.

We will examine each unique time that Peter's name is mentioned in the gospels. We will search the life lesson involved including the context and impact on both Peter and how it relates to us today. Each encounter also gives us insight into how God works with a man during his life time.

Perhaps even more telling is that Peter might best be understood as a barometer of the unfolding of just who Jesus is and how He reveals Himself to Mankind. Consistent with each of our life's journey we will see that the revelation of Jesus is progressive, beginning with our meeting Him where we are willing to receive Him, and continuing until our dying day.

While Jesus walked the earth He had emptied Himself of His Divinity. Meaning that He did not walk "as God" while on earth. He walked as a man. This means that the things He said and did could be done by anyone of us that are willing to walk with Him by His Spirit. When Jesus was on earth He did do the miraculous at times and He did it with the Power of the Holy Spirit that is also available to His followers here on earth.

There is what the Bible calls an "Anointing" that enables or releases things to be done on earth as they are done in Heaven. We will see that Peter recognized that "Anointing" more readily than any of the other disciples and jumped to participate in the anointing more quickly than the others. The name Messiah actually means the "Anointed One." And this is who the world was looking for at the time of Jesus. Unfortunately, because He did not come in the way or the fashion that was expected for the Messiah, so many missed the Messiah who came to live, suffer, and die and be resurrected again paying for our sins.

Also, unfortunately, the church often misses the working of the Anointing today. There are times when God is working in our midst and we either want to catalog it or observe it but are resistant to participating in it and gathering some of it into our own lives.

Getting ready for the call of God in someone's life can happen through family, friend, co-worker, or any myriad ways. I have concluded that the Holy Spirit prepares the soil of our heart when we show interest to ask, seek, or knock. He does not seem to barge in where He is unwelcome. But He will be found easily by seekers. Here we have an example of brothers and later some partners in fishing, that became a part of the core group of

Apostles. They evidently had been influenced by the preaching of John the Baptist and when John pointed to Jesus, one of these fishermen named Andrew quickly followed up and began talking with Jesus and introduced Him to his brother- Peter:

John 1:40-42 *One of the two who heard John* SPEAK, *and followed Him, was Andrew, Simon Peter's brother. He first found his own brother Simon, and said to him, "We have found the Messiah" (which is translated, the Christ). And he brought him to Jesus. Now when Jesus looked at him, He said, "You are Simon the son of Jonah. You shall be called Cephas" (which is translated, A Stone).*

THE CALL-PETER PERSONALLY TOUCHED TO FOLLOW JESUS.

Mat 4:18 *And Jesus, walking by the Sea of Galilee, saw two brothers, Simon called Peter, and Andrew his brother, casting a net into the sea; for they were fishermen.*

Luke 5:1-11 *So it was, as the multitude pressed about Him to hear the word of God, that He stood by the Lake of Gennesaret, and saw two boats standing by the lake; but the fishermen had gone from them and were washing* THEIR *nets. Then He got into one of the boats, which was Simon's, and asked him to put out a little from the land. And He sat down and taught the multitudes from the boat. When He had stopped speaking, He said to Simon, "Launch out into the deep and let down your nets for a catch." But Simon answered and said to Him, "Master, we have toiled all night and caught nothing; nevertheless at Your word I will let down the net." And when they had done this, they caught a great number of fish, and their net was breaking. So they signaled to* THEIR *partners in the other boat to come and help them. And they came and filled both the boats, so that they began to sink. When Simon Peter saw* IT, *he fell down at Jesus' knees, saying, "Depart from me, for I am a sinful man, O Lord!" For he and all who were with him were astonished at the catch of fish which they had taken; and so also* WERE *James and John, the sons of Zebedee, who were partners with Simon. And Jesus said to Simon, "Do not be afraid. From now on you will catch men." So when they had brought their boats to land, they forsook all and followed Him*

The call of Peter came while Peter was at work! - And it went like this. Peter had come in after a night of fishing- without catching anything. He and his partners were cleaning their nets. There were a throng of people on the shore and a man named Jesus was trying to talk to them all. Jesus imposed on Peter to borrow his boat and to take him a few yards out so Jesus could be heard by more people that were thronging Him. Jesus then preached and Peter had ears to hear the message of life. Jesus taught as one having authority. After the message was given, Jesus said to Peter to go out where it is deeper- let down your nets –the fish are there for the catching.

Now understand the dynamic. Not only had they caught no fish when the fishing was "supposed to be done." But in mid or late morning (depending on how long Jesus preached), there were no fish running at this time of day- every fisherman knew that. BUT Peter did not argue- Peter responded in obedience. He had just heard words of life- and now he was willing to hear words of direction.

When the boat filled with fish- and it took two boats to carry the load- Peter was overwhelmed with the outright miracle. Here was a Man who called forth fish out of their sleep to jump into Peter's nets! In the laws of fishing on the Sea of Galilee this had never happened- it was against all fishing rules of success. It was by nature against all normal results.

It would be like a surgeon closing up the body with cancer that he was unable to remove, only to have all traces of cancer found in subsequent tests-gone in Jesus name.

Notice the response of Peter- the miracle was so great to him that he knew he was in the presence of One who is Holy. Do you think Peter saw Jesus as Holy because he brought fish to the net? Let's consider the context. First of all we later learn that Peter and his brother were at a stage in life where they were looking for someone spiritual to come along to teach them. They were probably tired of the same old hypocritical teaching they got in church every Saturday. Secondly, Peter heard the sermon preached and it undoubtedly contained words of life, but also words proclaiming a Kingdom to come. Thirdly, consider that Peter had been fishing the Sea of Galilee all his life. His father was a fisherman. When you fish the same "sea" day after day and year after year you clearly know the ways of the sea. This is not like the ocean that the waves could bring in the miraculous on their own.

We would more likely call the Sea of Galilee a lake. You can see across it, it is basically self-contained with water coming in from the underground of Mt. Herman and going out in the Jordan River to the south towards Jericho. This means there is a rhythm to life in the Sea. Surely wind storms could be disruptive but that is about it. It was clear to Peter there was an intervention by Jesus to the normal rhythm. From Peter's perspective this intervention was all the evidence he needed to realize that only a heaven sent man could have this kind of power and authority.

Evidently Peter was a man under conviction. A man under conviction is looking for an opportunity to get sin off of his chest. Peter's revelation of who Jesus is at that moment brought life into perspective and a chance to clear his heart of his own sinful ways. Repentance was the first response to the Man sent by heaven.

Why did Jesus choose to reveal Himself as Holiness? Because what was evidently revealed to Peter was that he was in the presence of Holiness Himself and Peter's reaction was that he was a sinner. He was moved to repentance and humility. He suddenly was overwhelmed with the feeling of his personal failure and inadequacy.

Notice by response it was not cockiness, it was not how can I get you to go fishing with me more often, it was not how can I get this authority. But instead it was the human reaction that all the unsaved people of the world will one day have in the revealed Presence of Jesus Christ. It was a sense of not belonging. Just as Peter called out – I am a sinner and I don't belong around you.

Have we made Jesus out to be less than He is? We speak of His Presence as though it is an exciting and "feel good" thing. While it can be that - it is first humbling. While there may be joy first there is humility- I must bow down. I must recognize that He is Greatness and Love and Beauty such as has never been before.

Imagine the next words from the Mouth of Holiness Himself? From now on you will catch men and not fish! Without a clue as to what that meant or the ramifications of it - they dropped their nets, without stopping to finish cleaning them- they dropped their fish without even selling them - they quit their vocation to follow this Man! It is the question of the ages- the question to every human being that ever lived.

Will you follow this Man?

While Jesus later on explains what it means to follow Him - deny yourself, take up your own cross bearing the burden of the Kingdom of God here on earth during the age of the church - He said none of those things here. Here the revelation spoke for itself - and regardless of the cost – it struck the core of Peter and others that there was no choice – they found their reason for their existence.

They forsook all they had and did to follow this Man. Choosing to accept Jesus is a critical first step to finding life. It is vital to see here that Peter was on a quest. He was searching for life answers. He was not caught up in catching and selling fish. He was not merely living on earth letting time go by. He was after something or someone from above.

He heard Jesus speak and something stirred deep down in that place that only God can touch. We all have a hole in our soul. We may try to fill it with the things of this world but those things always fall short. We try to fill it with success, fame, or fortune – but these things leave even a bigger hole.

When Jesus taught that day, standing on a boat a few yards from shore, He spoke words of life.

DISCUSSION CHAPTER ONE
THE CALL OF PETER

1) Describe the circumstances of the initial request.

2) Why it was a big deal that they caught fish after Jesus told them where to go and what to do?

3) Describe fully Peter's reaction – his revelation of Jesus, his reaction to Jesus, his willingness to leave all.

4) Did Peter have any idea what it meant to catch men rather than fish?

5) Why would they follow Jesus?

CHAPTER TWO
PETER TAPPING INTO
THE ANOINTING

<u>Matt. 14:26-32</u> *And when the disciples saw Him walking on the sea, they were troubled, saying, "It is a ghost!" And they cried out for fear. But immediately Jesus spoke to them, saying, "Be of good cheer! It is I; do not be afraid." And Peter answered Him and said, "Lord, if it is You, command me to come to You on the water." So He said, "Come." And when Peter had come down out of the boat, he walked on the water to go to Jesus. But when he saw that the wind* WAS *boisterous, he was afraid; and beginning to sink he cried out, saying, "Lord, save me!" And immediately Jesus stretched out* HIS *hand and caught him, and said to him, "O you of little faith, why did you doubt?" And when they got into the boat, the wind ceased.*

When the topic of Jesus and Peter walking on water is discussed, often there is a mocking of Peter. Many accuse Peter of failing. Let's take a closer look. Peter is fascinated by the exercise of Jesus' power over nature. The disciples were witnessing the most remarkable thing they had ever seen.

In fact this is one of the most famous examples of the power of God working in a man - the walking on water. There are silly explanations e.g. the water was shallow, and He walked on stones - yet more non-believers are familiar with this event than even the raising of Jairus' daughter from the dead.

But the account is clear - they were out in the middle of the Sea, 80 feet or so deep, and the waves were kicking up, and all the disciples saw what they could not quite comprehend. They guessed as to what it was - a spirit- then they heard the now familiar voice – be happy it is Me – don't be afraid.

Before we deal with Peter's revelation let us clearly understand what Jesus was doing. First of all, Jesus never did anything while He was on earth as God. Everything He did – miracles, casting out demons, healing the sick, raising the dead were all done as Jesus the man. The significance of this point is that when Jesus became aware of an anointing available to take action in or with, He acted. In other words, these heavenly interventions while Jesus was on earth were inspired and empowered from the Holy Spirit. What is the significance of this truth to us?

<u>Romans 8:11</u> *But if the Spirit of Him who raised Jesus from the dead dwells in you, He who raised Christ from the dead will also give life to your mortal bodies through His Spirit who dwells in you.*

The first time Jesus "acted as God" was not until after His resurrection. He materialized through the locked door in the upper room where the disciples were eating and wondering what was next. All of His earthly time was as a man walking and finding the Power of God to do everything that He was inspired to do.

Now to Peter, he had been with Jesus enough that somehow he knew he could participate and exercise himself in the Power of God just as he saw Jesus do it. This is one of the most misunderstood facts of life by the church today. There is a "spectator" mentality that even in the church we want to talk about what Jesus did, vacillating between doubt and wonder whether He really did those things literally, and not even letting ourselves imagine that we COULD do them let alone that we SHOULD do them.

That's right! The church should be a place where the miraculous is a normal part of the life of a church. If it is not – take inventory – and find out what shelf the miraculous has been left on, take it out and dust it off – and exercise it back into regular practice. It seems we are waiting for Jesus to again perform and do the miraculous for us. When in truth He is waiting for us to step out and do the miraculous ourselves. Our theology these days is waiting for Jesus to barge in on our lives and perform like at a circus. Our theology is wrong.

We will see later that the disciples in the book of Acts did not wait for a Holy interruption to bring forth the miraculous. They were able to see what God would want done and do it themselves. Now let's go back to the walking on the water.

Jesus was walking on the water via an anointing or enablement that gave Him heavenly power to not be subject to gravity for this event. He sought to catch up to his disciples who were following his orders and in a boat going to the other side. Peter recognized the anointing that Jesus was walking in and he wanted to participate or take part in that anointing.

It is interesting to note that Peter's faith to walk on water would be released to action if Jesus would just tell him to do so. So **all Peter felt he needed was a word from Jesus** and he could walk in the anointing on the water himself. Well Jesus gave him the Word – not complicated, not a formula, just *come* - and Peter jumped out to start walking on water himself. The curious aspect to the event was that Peter did not ask for the water to calm down first - and just as curious Jesus did not calm it down first!

With the wind "boisterous" and obviously the waves a swirling, Peter started to look around at the circumstances only after he got out of the boat. He suddenly realized the circumstances he found himself in and got scared. He did not start to sink until he could no longer walk in the anointing and stand on the Word. As he started to sink he cried out for help and Jesus reached out and grabbed him and they both got into the boat.

Note Jesus did not say "nice try Peter, maybe next time!" Rather He admonished Peter (or scolded him) -"o ye of little faith" – why doubt? Was Jesus being too hard on Peter? Well first let's acknowledge that Jesus may be as hard on us as He deems necessary. But no, Jesus was not hard on him by saying you asked for the Word, I gave it to you, and you let doubt creep in. Doubt kills our faith. Doubt and unbelief are the cancer to faith in the life of a believer. **Jesus would have none of it – He would not tolerate it** – and He is the same yesterday, today, and forever. In other words, He will not tolerate it today!

How often we are faced with troubled waters in the midst of our Word of promise? The chief enemy is doubt and unbelief. Did you ever notice that in the troubles of life we look around and only see the troubles? What would happen if we would ignore the circumstances and protect the anointing and cling to the word given to us by Jesus in faith?

There is a prevailing negativity in the world. Negativity – things won't work, or that will never happen, or that will never happen for me, etc. – is a breeding ground for doubt and unbelief. Let's face it – if the challenge is to jump 10 feet and you jump 9 it is a failure. If you jump 10 – then why did you not jump 11 feet. If you jump 11 feet – oh that wasn't so hard I bet anybody can jump that far. There is a prevailing air of negativity that wants to accuse everyone in every situation that we are failing or that we are not good enough.

Some of the greatest achievers in this world fight doubt and unbelief daily. Any record holder will tell you that what they had to overcome was not the elements or the opponent but that inner man who kept looking for reasons why failure was certain.

James says a double minded man is unstable in all of his ways and receives nothing from the Lord. Pretty strong stuff – is our prayer life mired in doubt? Today is the day to get rid of it. Confess your doubts and unbelief and claim in faith that which is yours. Faith is the "substance" of things hoped for the evidence of things to come. Faith is something to get a hold of, it is not wishful thinking. When faith is experienced hope is realized whether it has literally shown up or not. To the believer he can "see it and hold onto it" even before the literal manifestation.

There was a man who brought his son to Jesus for deliverance – because the disciples could not help him. Jesus told the father – believe and your son will be delivered.

Mark 9:24 *So He said to them, "This kind can come out by nothing but prayer and fasting."*

His son was set free in that moment - the father brought what faith he had and asked Jesus to make up any deficit. That is the way of Jesus. Bring what you have-He will make up the difference.

If the walking on water event took place today, I can just imagine what the church would say. Why didn't Jesus calm the waters first, that wasn't fair; why not give Peter a chance to walk on calm waters and then maybe next time stir the waters? We always want to make excuses; we want to justify ourselves and others. But this confrontation with doubt and unbelief and others like it during the ministry of Jesus on earth are for the benefit of the church. In fact no where do I see Jesus say, "You need to be smarter, be tougher, or be stronger", or for that matter He never prodded anyone on any physical or mental shortcomings. Jesus had made it very clear that the number one enemy of the believer is doubt and fear. And He won't tolerate it!

As you look forward in life just know that negative thoughts and feelings are there. My Pastor says that FEAR is the False Evidence that Appears Real. This is a good summary to wage the battle for victory in the life of all believers. In fact, we are known as "believers" yet we have a tendency to wallow in doubt and unbelief. Let's live up to our name.

Before we leave this chapter let's turn the whole account upside down! This was a spectacular event – in fact where ever you go today most non believers know the story of the walking on water by Jesus. How did He do it? Well an "Anointing" came on Him – an infusion of the Holy Spirit enabled Jesus to walk on the water. Maybe the reason Peter did not bother asking about the storm was that he was enamored with recognizing the "Anointing," and he wanted "in on it!" Maybe this account has nothing to do with troubled times and everything to do with the times of the Anointing.

Maybe the issue was that all of the disciples should have "jumped out of the boat." Maybe they all should have demanded to come and meet Jesus in the anointing that He was flowing in. Peter, as many of them were, was a fisherman. It was not the first boisterous sea he had ever been on. His thoughts were not on the wind blowing until he thought of the wind and lost the anointing to walk on the water. Jesus got upset that Peter "lost the anointing," and he lost it through doubt and unbelief. The anointing is a fragile experience on the human level. It is easily lost when distractions come and our minds wander. Oh that we would renounce our tendency to be spectators only – and that we would be on the alert, when the anointing comes that we would jump out of the boat.

We must regard each of these events in the lives of the disciples as vital to their training. That is right. These twelve men were being trained to start the church of Jesus Christ after the resurrection and Jesus planned each event as a training exercise. Jesus was going to take twelve "unlearned" men to start the church. He only had three years or so to get these guys ready and each noted event was a critical milestone in their education.

This makes it imperative that each of us begins to accept the fact we are on a lifelong training mission. When significant events take place we can begin to recognize the milestones for what they are. Crucial learning times to be used to advance the Kingdom of God here on earth.

Discussion Chapter Two
Peter Tapping into the Anointing

1) What was the first reaction of the disciples of seeing Jesus walking on water?

2) Fishermen most likely had seen sudden storms many times as you consider the geography of the Sea of Galilee.

3) Why didn't all the disciples jump out of the boat?

4) Describe the type of personality of Peter revealed here.

5) What is the difference in seeing the waves from the boat and walking in the waves?

6) Was Jesus hard on Peter?

CHAPTER THREE
PETER LEARNS THE
QUALIFICATIONS OF
LEADERSHIP

<u>Matt 11:10-20</u> *When He had called the multitude to* HIMSELF, *He said to them, "Hear and understand: Not what goes into the mouth defiles a man; but what comes out of the mouth, this defiles a man." Then His disciples came and said to Him, "Do You know that the Pharisees were offended when they heard this saying?" But He answered and said, "Every plant which My heavenly Father has not planted will be uprooted. Let them alone. They are blind leaders of the blind. And if the blind leads the blind, both will fall into a ditch." Then Peter answered and said to Him, "Explain this parable to us." So Jesus said, "Are you also still without understanding? Do you not yet understand that whatever enters the mouth goes into the stomach and is eliminated? But those things which proceed out of the mouth come from the heart, and they defile a man. For out of the heart proceed evil thoughts, murders, adulteries, fornications, thefts, false witness, blasphemies. These are* THE THINGS *which defile a man, but to eat with unwashed hands does not defile a man."*

<u>1 Samuel 16:7</u> *But the LORD said to Samuel, "Do not look at his appearance or at his physical stature, because I have refused him. For* THE LORD DOES *not* SEE *as man sees; for*

man looks at the outward appearance, but the LORD looks at the heart."

First of all Jesus fights back against those that try to impose the appearance of religion. Those that take offense at someone not following some manmade religious rules were a great irritation to Jesus. He says to His disciples in effect, "If they want to be offended let them – they are blind and are not a part of what I am bringing to the earth."

If we look over the 3 ½ years of Jesus' ministry on earth we will see Him regularly riled up against complaining religious hierarchy. He had no tolerance for outward rules running the faith!

This Biblical principle is clear in that it says, "man looks on the outward appearance, but God looks at the heart." In other words, human kind is pre-occupied with what they see outwardly when they look at a man (or even more likely a woman), while God looks for what is going on in the heart. On earth we are enamored with appearance and accomplishment and make our judgments on people accordingly.

When the children of Israel demanded from Samuel that God give them a king like other people groups had, it is interesting to note that God sent Samuel to the smallest tribe where he found the man who was a "head taller" than any other man in Israel, and said he was to be made king.

The demand for a king was interpreted by Samuel as a rejection of his prophetic abilities to let the people know the mind of God. But God said it is not about you Samuel it is about how they perceive their relationship with me. But the biggest man proved to be a man who did not have a "heart right relationship" with God. In fact, King Saul labored all the time in the perceptions of others, in doubt and unbelief, and constant fear that his position as king was doomed. He was constantly disobedient to the word of the Lord and one day God said enough is enough. King Saul was the poster child for negative thinking and the cancerous effects it can have on our lives.

Although to the successor it seemed to take a long time for Saul to be dethroned, his removal was certain and just a matter of time. A confluence of events had to take place first.

1 Samuel 13:14 *But now your kingdom shall not continue. The LORD has sought for Himself a man after His own heart, and the LORD has commanded him to be commander over His people, because you have not kept what the LORD commanded you."*

Act 13:22 *And when he had removed him, he raised up unto them David to be their king; to whom also he gave testimony, and said, I have found David the [son] of Jesse, a man after mine own heart, which shall fulfil all my will.*

The king that followed Saul was just the opposite. Oddly, in appearance he was handsome, and he was accomplished – while Saul killed his thousands, David killed his tens of thousands – but the true measurement of the man was that "he was a man after God's own heart".

Notice in the 1 Sam. 13:14 verse that God is not looking for the smartest, biggest, strongest, and best looking- BUT He is looking for a man that has a heart for God. In this computer age we live in every time you want to "Google" someone – or search for a job for example – you are best served by doing a "key words" search that describes the criteria you are looking for in a job. In other words, search for that which is most important to you. God's primary search criterion is "the condition of the heart."

My friends as David found out and as Peter and the disciples found out – it is all about the condition and motivation of the heart that makes you eligible to serve God.

In the New Testament text at the beginning of this chapter Jesus is teaching that the rules about what goes into the mouth are meaningless. In earlier history the rules were there for health sake not for God sake. But as food preparation improved these rules lost their meaning for health – but they were never intended to reflect their heart relationship with God. Here Jesus drives home the teaching point of what takes priority.

He is teaching that what comes out of the mouth reflects what is in the heart. And what mankind is faced with is a heart clean up not a hand clean up. That defilement was no longer measured in *"health terms"* – as in you will get sick if you put that in your mouth – but now defilement was measured in *"spirit terms"* that if that comes out of your mouth this means that your heart has sickness that needs cleansing.

Defilement is an issue long lost on the psyche of the western church. We have so watered down the value of purity that not only do Christians have the same percentage of premarital sex as unbelievers but that one out of six abortions are done by "believers." Holiness and purity in America are basically considered "fringe or radical" teaching. The prevailing perception is that those were important in the past and unattainable in the present.

Isaiah had been a prophet with access to the king on a regular basis. He walked in the uppermost ranks of both church and palace and had authority in both. One day the king died and Isaiah was "in prayer." The Spirit of God evidently tore back the curtain separating heaven from earth and allowed Isaiah to "see into" the events going on around the throne. They were certainly awe inspiring

Isaiah 6:1-7 In the year that King Uzziah died, I saw the Lord sitting on a throne, high and lifted up, and the train of His ROBE *filled the temple. Above it stood seraphim; each one had six wings: with two he covered his face, with two he covered his feet, and with two he flew. And one cried to another and said: "Holy, holy, holy* IS *the LORD of hosts; The whole earth* IS *full of His glory!" And the posts of the door were shaken by the voice of him who cried out, and the house was filled with smoke. So I said: "Woe* IS *me, for I am undone! Because I* AM *a man of unclean lips, And I dwell in the midst of a people of unclean lips; For my eyes have seen the King, The LORD of hosts." Then one of the seraphim flew to me, having in his hand a live coal* WHICH *he had taken with the tongs from the altar. And he touched my mouth* WITH IT, *and said: "Behold, this has touched your lips; Your iniquity is taken away, And your sin purged."*

Isaiah, the man who had been prophesying regularly before this – that is speaking for God to both king and subject – suddenly realized he was a man of unclean lips! I wonder if it took the death of the king and the threat to his position when a new king took over to prepare Isaiah to look into the condition of his own heart. After all, with the king dead, the new king could come in and get rid of all advisers to the previous king – including his spiritual adviser.

In any event, in that moment he realized that while he had been speaking things heard from heaven all along in his ministry – he suddenly realized he did not personally measure up to the task. He realized his own unworthiness, his own defilement on the words he spoke. Even though the things he said in God's name were from God he suddenly realized that the vessel used to proclaim them was unclean. Isaiah himself was that unclean vessel. Once more, there was recognition by Isaiah that the root cause of his uncleanness had never been dealt with. The angel had to take away the "iniquity" or the root of it.

In the course of the revelation of defilement, God used an angel to clear and clean those lips. Immediately afterwards **God allowed Isaiah to overhear a discussion around the throne** of His desire to find a man to send into a situation as His representative. Isaiah – freshly cleaned up – immediately volunteered to be that man.

Isaiah 6:8-10 *Also I heard the voice of the Lord, saying: "Whom shall I send, And who will go for Us?" Then I said, "Here AM I! Send me." And He said, "Go, and tell this people: 'Keep on hearing, but do not understand; Keep on seeing, but do not perceive.' "Make the heart of this people dull, And their ears heavy, And shut their eyes; Lest they see with their eyes, And hear with their ears, And understand with their heart, And return and be healed."*

Imagine the privilege of being allowed to hear God in discussion. But notice God needed to clean up the vessel before the assignment could be granted. Also note that Isaiah volunteered before he knew what the task was. Since this passage of scripture is a rare look into the way of God in heaven, let us learn from it.

We have a tendency to assume that God has it all planned out (that is everything He wants done on earth), and that we are just pawns on the board called earth. Well this passage (and Job chapter one) refutes that kind of thinking. This passage shows that God is looking among His choice for who has gotten her or himself ready for the task. Noah was ready, Abraham was ready, 40 years later Moses was ready, and so forth. By the same token Lot was not ready and therefore cities were destroyed by judgment (see below).

We learn much here. God evidently will use even defiled people at times for certain situations. But at the same time He needs to find those pure vessels for strategic work in the Kingdom here on earth. Was there ever a time when the need was greater for those pure vessels to do the work of the Kingdom than here and now?

Another key learning point here is that God "needs" men and women on earth! You say God doesn't need anyone - he can make the rocks cry out. Yes He can "choose" do anything, anyway He wants to at any time. But God has evidently "chosen" to use men and women to be His vessels on earth during the church age to take up key positions of influence and work in the lives of nations, cities, families, and individuals.

This is where the application of scripture that says, "many are called but few are chosen," comes into perspective. He has called many to intervene in the course of human history but only a few were undefiled and useable. Consider the words of Jesus when He said, "O Capernaum, if the works done in you had been done in Sodom and Gomorrah those cities would be standing today!" If you and I would ask then why weren't those works done in Sodom and Gomorrah- the answer was God could not find a man to do the works that needed done.

Abraham had tried to intercede on their behalf and the Lord was willing to spare those cities if there were 10 "righteous" people found there. Righteous is defined as people that had faith in God. Lot and his wife, and 2 virgin daughters, 2 sons in law, married to 2 other daughters and 2 other sons equals 10!

If Lot had been able to keep all the members of his family in the faith, Sodom and Gomorrah would have been saved.

For a little side light let's consider why the Lord said:

Gen 18:21 *I will go down now and see whether they have done altogether according to the outcry against it that has come to Me; and if not, I will know."*

Obviously the Lord already knew how depraved these cities were. Why the visitation before the judgment of destruction? The angels were going to visit and be seen by the people who would look upon them and have an opportunity to see the "beauty of the Lord" and be motivated to repent by being able to compare their own ugliness of sin and depravation with that beauty. Instead, when the people of the city saw for themselves that "beauty" they were so hardened in their hearts toward sin they lusted after the angels.

Sadly, even the household of Lot was unable to find their own repentance so the judgment was carried out.

2 Peter 2:6-8 *and turning the cities of Sodom and Gomorrah into ashes, condemned* THEM *to destruction, making* THEM *an example to those who afterward would live ungodly; and delivered righteous Lot,* WHO WAS *oppressed by the filthy conduct of the wicked (for that righteous man, dwelling among them, tormented* HIS *righteous soul from day to day by seeing and hearing* THEIR *lawless deeds*

Lot himself was just, but he could not maintain the leadership it took to save his household. Notice that the constant battle of Lot was the manner of living surrounding his every move in life. He lived in a world where sin abounded and while he found the grace to personally survive his influence over others was minimal.

Let's be clear on the point, God puts His will out for who will hear it. Many may hear what God wants done but only a few will have prepared themselves to be eligible to do it. Let's look at Esther as a clear example of this kind of approach to understanding how God works in life on earth.

Esther 4: 10-16 *Then Esther spoke to Hathach, and gave him a command for Mordecai: "All the king's servants and the people of the king's provinces know that any man or woman who goes into the inner court to the king, who has not been called,* HE HAS *but one law: put* ALL *to death, except the one to whom the king holds out the golden scepter, that he may live. Yet I myself have not been called to go in to the king these thirty days." So they told Mordecai Esther's words. And Mordecai told* THEM *to answer Esther: "Do not think in your heart that you will escape in the king's palace any more than all the other Jews. For if you remain completely silent at this time, relief and deliverance will arise for the Jews from another place, but you and your father's house will perish.* **Yet who knows whether you have come to the kingdom for** SUCH *a time as this?" Then Esther told* THEM *to reply to Mordecai: "Go, gather all the Jews who are present in Shushan, and fast for me; neither eat nor drink for three days, night or day.* **My maids and I will fast likewise. And so I will go to the king, which** IS **against the law; and if I perish, I perish!"**

Her uncle was saying to her if you don't go before the king and intercede on behalf of the Jews God has prepared others to step in. You see we are not pawns on the chess board of life, we have free choice, and although we may have been positioned to perform the will of God we are not the only ones in position to accomplish that which God wants done.

When Alexander Graham Bell put in his patent for the telephone – hours later – yes, hours later! – Elisha Gray put in a patent with almost the identical drawing for a patent for the telephone. What am I saying? God had released the plans to improve the communications on earth, and two men rose to the occasion, put what they thought were their plans on paper and went to get the patent - and were only hours apart.

My friends we think the Kingdom is about us. It is not, it is about Him and His plans and His will, and His timing for things to take place. Our job is to make ourselves eligible, to get ourselves clean, deal with root causes of iniquity, get ourselves ready, and listen for His words of direction.

Why are churches started all over the world? Because many are listening and hearing that God wants this kind or that kind of church to be available for this group or that group or this village or that neighborhood.

Get yourself ready! We must nourish and harbor a group of pure vessels in the church- those that will keep themselves from all manner of sin and defilement. We for some reason are trying to make church be "fun for the kids." Oh that we would learn ourselves and teach others the value of preparation to serve God in any field of endeavor.

If you are going to be a lawyer you must go to under graduate school, attain a certain level of performance and graduate successfully. Then you apply to law school, and you are competing for entry with those that also graduated successfully from other under graduate schools. You also take a graduate school test. Then let's say for a school like Harvard Law School you are compared with all the other students who are applying. Only those students that have made themselves the "most eligible" to succeed by taking the right courses, with the right grades, taken the common tests and scored high, and have demonstrated skills beyond schoolwork will be accepted.

We have misunderstood how the Kingdom of God works here on earth. Just because the church will accept any and all – does not mean that just any and all can do the strategic work in the Kingdom that God wants done on the earth. We must become pure vessels who make themselves eligible, who keep themselves in faith seeking God with all their heart, with their entire mind, and with all their soul.

When Peter asked for further explanation in our text of this chapter, he was coming from the "religious thinking of the day." There was such a false sense that if I do everything outwardly correct then I am correct! Jesus, who had laid out the New Testament agenda in the Sermon on the Mount, was refuting the conventional wisdom of the day. Just as Jesus had redefined murder- that murder is not just when someone kills another – but murder also takes place when you hate another. So Jesus is giving a New Testament definition of how to become eligible to be used in God's Kingdom.

Sometimes it is just as important to see what is not important as it to see what is important. Jesus says – and this is vital for all the church age – that the outside of the vessel is irrelevant. It is what is on the inside. This then makes every living person a candidate to be used mightily in the Kingdom of God here on earth. It does not matter what you look like – short, tall, skinny, fat, handsome, ugly, black, brown, yellow, white, or blue!

Each candidate is required to clean the inside of the vessel! How do we do that? Repent, live a life in fear before a Holy God. Realize that we must give an account for every word spoken, and every deed done!

We live in a day of generic drugs. This means that drug producers use the same formulas to make a drug, but don't use the advertised name for it. The "thinking" is that it is the same drug, but can cost less because they don't pay as much for packaging and advertising.

What they don't tell you is that the advertised name brand also has stricter guidelines and standards for production. So that before the advertised name is put on the drug these production standards must be adhered to. Such is not the case with generic drugs, so there are quality issues and different ingredients that come in to play.

The same is true of "private label" foods. If you open a can of Green Giant green beans, and open a can of private brand green beans and dump them out you will see the Green Giant brand will have beans that are standardized size and shape. The private brand will have ends of the beans, and various size and shapes. Yes they are both cans of beans but the second can cannot bear the name of Green Giant because they don't measure up to the standards of that name.

In the 21st century we are living in a "Generic Christian Church Age." We have lost all understanding of what the standards are. We have ordained those living in sin and call it tolerance. We think we can private label Christianity, but when you open the can and dump out the ingredients, we see that which is aberrant to God. We have reduced BOTH the inward standards and the outward standards. Let us be clear and say it again – all sinners are welcome to come to the Church of Jesus Christ. But the inward standards will be taught and the expectation for *all to change* as a result of walking with Jesus will happen.

Isn't it true if you give your child an inch they will take a mile? Jesus in redefining who is eligible to serve in God's Kingdom, was clearly dropping the "outward" standards that man wants to enforce. But He did not drop the inward requirements for cleansing. In fact, Jesus was emphasizing the focus on the standards of inward cleansing of all defilement.

In the Generic Church, we want to drop all standards – both outward and inward. But this is not deserving of the Name-Christianity.

Discussion Chapter Three
Peter Learns the Qualifications of Leadership

---

1) Describe the difference between what goes in and what comes out.

2) Where does "what comes out" come from? And what does it tell us.

3) Do we have a responsibility to "get ourselves ready?"

4) How do we get ourselves ready?

5) Describe Isaiah's encounter in heaven.

6) What do we learn from Ester's choice?

7) What is a generic Christian?

CHAPTER FOUR
THOU ART THE CHRIST

<u>Mark 8:27-33</u> *Now Jesus and His disciples went out to the towns of Caesarea Philippi; and on the road He asked His disciples, saying to them, "Who do men say that I am?" So they answered, "John the Baptist; but some SAY, Elijah; and others, one of the prophets." He said to them, "But who do you say that I am?" Peter answered and said to Him, "You are the Christ."*

Then He strictly warned them that they should tell no one about Him. And He began to teach them that the Son of Man must suffer many things, and be rejected by the elders and chief priests and scribes, and be killed, and after three days rise again. He spoke this word openly. Then Peter took Him aside and began to rebuke Him. But when He had turned around and looked at His disciples, He rebuked Peter, saying, "Get behind Me, Satan! For you are not mindful of the things of God, but the things of men."

This is the 4th time that Peter is mentioned chronologically, and it is certainly one of the most profound revelations by a person in the Bible. This was a highlight moment- a milestone- in the life of the disciples including Peter foremost. At the same time it represented a sign to Jesus that his disciples were finally making themselves more available to revelation from heaven. There is an order and progression of revelation in the Kingdom of God. Up until this moment in the journey of the followers of Jesus the disciples were still trying to sort out all the wonders and wisdom of this Man. There was uncertainty as to exactly who He was. Maybe until this moment his greatness was understood in human terms only – what a gifted and great man is Jesus – in the eyes of His followers.

But as the journey progressed and the more they "saw" of Jesus, their hearts opened further to the understanding that He was beyond human. We have to understand that the Jews since the days of Moses looked for the Messiah. The greatness and power of the Messiah that was expected was wrapped in grandeur and not humility. So that when Jesus walked on the earth it was a complete paradigm shift that the Messiah could possibly be wrapped in swaddling clothes and lying in a manger because there was no room for Him in the inn. They had been looking for the Messiah to come in all His grandeur and missed the need that He should come first to be humble and die and then secondly come in grandeur and all glory.

This paradox could not be reconciled in the minds of Jews while Jesus walked on earth. They, at this time, had trouble comprehending the need for Jesus to first accomplish the cleansing role of the Sacrificial Lamb.

But God so loved the world that He sent His only Begotten Son full of grace and truth. Jesus had to first establish himself as worthy via perfection in a human vessel with all its limitations and facing all of our human temptations. Then He had to endure the role of Savior by giving up His life for us. Then He had to be resurrected and seated on the right hand of the throne. And only then the grandeur of the coming King would have His day.

Basically every Jew just wanted and expected the Messiah to go right to the throne in grandeur – period.

But in the spirit realm of human kind there is a capacity to hear and see from heaven. Evidently at this juncture of the journey, Jesus wanted to hear if they could articulate that He was heaven sent and not just another "great man." When Peter articulated that Jesus was the Messiah, there was a personal rejoicing by Jesus (literally, Jesus jumped for joy and twirled and danced). Understanding that Jesus is the Messiah is not comprehended intellectually. It is not based on a human deduction. Rather it is like a light bulb that goes on. It is like when someone says, "Oh, I see it now. Or, I get it now."

In the progression of revelation, it was important that they understood that this was a Spiritual journey and not a political journey. Neither was this a religious journey, to reorganize the Jewish hierarchy. They could not be ready to be told the next step until they understood the real agenda of God - that this was the hour for God to express His love to mankind by sending the Sacrificial Messiah.

When they could express their understanding that Jesus was the Messiah they then showed that they were tuning into heaven and that they were beginning to show capacity to be ready to receive spiritual instructions. Jesus had been evidently "dying to tell them" that a tremendous perplexing event was going to take place. Immediately upon their revelation that He was the Messiah, Jesus went into disclosing and helping the disciples to plan for the day that He would die. He knew the potential damage His death could do to the Cause. He had never told them about His death until they demonstrated their understanding that He was in fact the Messiah. He knew they would have trouble getting their minds around His need to die.

Immediately Peter took issue with the foretelling. After all it is not logical. If you are here to set up the Kingdom - death of the King goes against anything that makes any sense at all. Well, as only Jesus can do – in the same conversation He praises Peter for hearing from heaven and accepting what he heard – and then condemns Peter for speaking for Satan. One moment Peter is grasping heavenly truth and then he processes the next spiritual step as not making any sense. And that is the point. Making sense is just that - processing spiritual truth in the 5 senses hardly ever makes "sense."

Here Jesus is all excited to help the disciples take another key step forward in their leadership training – after all He was preparing them to start the Church of Jesus Christ and evangelize the world – and Peter has to spoil the moment. Jesus is direct and has no political correctness about Him. He calls Peter a name and tells him to get behind him. That is the only place Satan should ever be in our life-behind us.

It was very important for Jesus to clear the air without apology or compromise. He is telling the group that their leadership must be ruled by the Spirit and not by what pleases any senses, like feels good, or seems right. He is showing that the Plan of God entails more than feel good, seems right to me, or I agree with that, kind of thinking. A good general rule is that if the world would approve it God would not and vice versa.

Whatever is conventional thinking then is usually the opposite of what God is thinking.

But the real point of this stage of the journey is coming to grips with the revelation – Jesus is the Messiah. In this age we generally don't think in terms of "needing" a Messiah. Rather we are in the age where people don't realize they need outside intervention and provision. We are most likely to think in terms of "what do I need to do?"

Our age is quickly losing the reality of the need for an advocate and substitute for our sins, probably because we don't take our sin very seriously. We gloss over the import of purity with thinking that the fact that "we all do it" makes it no big deal. In the church we are so busy trying to accommodate the culture that we are offering a Gospel that is so inclusive that anything goes.

Lost is the message that anyone can come in, but don't plan on staying that way! The world wants us to include homosexuals for example, so that we do not judge them, and let them come into our churches and stay the way they are. Somehow the truth has been so culturally watered down that we think anyone should be allowed in and allowed to stay the way they are. If that is the case why bother to come in?

No – here is reality. Each and every one of us is a sinner. Homosexuals, liars, thieves, adulterers, and the lists go on. There is no amount of good works we can do to compensate for our sins. Each and every one of us needs a substitute or a Savior, or a Messiah to take our place and pay our price for our sins. God requires it. And God provided for it through His Son.

The way of life is profoundly simple and yet the deceiving power of the heart of man makes it seem so complicated.

What is little understood in this regard is the difference in consequences about different sins. For example, lying is a sin. Should liars be allowed into the church? I hope so otherwise I could not get in. BUT once in- the church will minister to my lying tendencies so that I can find freedom from lying. Should homosexuals be allowed into the church? I also hope so for their sake. BUT again, once in the church then the church needs to minister to them to help them find their freedom.

Unfortunately, like it or not there are more consequences and difficulties for the homosexual. To get some insight consider this. If I walk into a store without a gun and in a threatening manner because of my size tell the store clerk to give me all the money and they do it – that is called robbery and if caught I may get 3 to 5 years. If I have a gun and stick it in the clerk's face and force them to open the cash drawer and take the money, now it is armed robbery. Now I will get 15 to 20 years. Why are the consequences so different? Because there is the possibility of permanent damage to the clerk if I should pull the trigger that could result in maiming or even death.

With homosexuality the reason we politically want to interpret it as we were "born that way" is the difficulty in getting free from it. The practice of it plays havoc on the psyche and soul of the practitioner as to damage and re route as it were the God given signals in the mind and body of people. The triggers for pleasure, wants and desires gets perverted in their application and it takes a mercy and grace from the power of the Holy Spirit to close off learned trigger points and redevelop them into their originally designed fashion.

Now when the liar comes into the church, first of all, that person knows he is a liar. He does not need anyone else to tell him he is a liar. Secondly, it takes liars (and all sinners) time to come to grips with their lying or their own sinful tendency whatever it may be. Often the blatant lies get dealt with through repentance and then practice in living out through experience freedom from lying. Depending on how ingrained the practice is in the liar's life the various shades or degrees of lying get dealt with often like peeling an onion.

In other words, lying can be dealt with by degrees. The most obvious first - down to the "little white lies" last. Let me quickly say that freedom, or deliverance, from lying can happen in one fell swoop by the Power of the Holy Spirit, and it's done with once and for all. But usually it is a process. The church must have the patience and forbearance to love the person in the process. Likewise the journey for the homosexual can be long and arduous. It has been said to all of us – God loves us so much He will not leave us the way He found us!

Let's face it the human condition is such that everyone knows something is missing in their life. There is a hole in our heart that keeps showing up no matter how we try to fill that hole with pleasure or gain. The hole can only be filled by one called by Peter the Messiah. The Christ comes in and fills that hole in our heart and helps us unite in heart and spirit with God the Father

The revelation of "thou art the Christ (Messiah)," is paramount to coming to grips with the truth that we need a substitute. We need someone to take our place. The world seems to accept the fact that Jesus lived and died and rose from the grave – but the world has trouble realizing He did it for each and every one of us and without it we have no place with God.

Outline Chapter Four
Thou Art the Christ

1) How did Peter know Jesus is the Messiah?

2) Why did Peter take exception to Jesus speaking about His coming death?

3) How would you describe a revelation from heaven?

4) How would you describe a revelation from Satan?

5) Why is there a need in the western church to accommodate those who acknowledge their shortcomings but don't want to change?

6) What is God's plan for the church and who does He want to come in and what does He want after they are in?

CHAPTER FIVE
PETER PARTICIPATES IN THE POWER OF AGREEMENT

<u>Luke 8:49– 56</u> *While He was still speaking, someone came from the ruler of the synagogue's* HOUSE, *saying to him, "Your daughter is dead. Do not trouble the Teacher." But when Jesus heard* IT, *He answered him, saying, "Do not be afraid; only believe, and she will be made well." When He came into the house, He permitted no one to go in except Peter, James, and John, and the father and mother of the girl. Now all wept and mourned for her; but He said, "Do not weep; she is not dead, but sleeping." And they ridiculed Him, knowing that she was dead. But He put them all outside, took her by the hand and called, saying, "Little girl, arise." Then her spirit returned, and she arose immediately. And He commanded that she be given* SOMETHING *to eat. And her parents were astonished, but He charged them to tell no one what had happened.*

A little understood principle in working God's will on earth is the power of agreement. We often think that Jesus will do whatever He wants anytime regardless of human involvement. But what we don't realize is that that is not how He works on earth during the church age. People can and do influence or restrain the use of the Power of God on earth. It is also time to consider this event in light of the fact that Jesus did not raise this girl from the dead as God. He did it as the man Jesus utilizing His faith in the Power of the Holy Spirit.

<u>Mark 6:1-6</u> *Then He went out from there and came to His own country, and His disciples followed Him. And when the Sabbath had come, He began to teach in the synagogue. And many hearing* HIM *were astonished, saying, "Where* DID *this Man* GET *these things? And what wisdom* IS *this which is given to Him, that such mighty works are performed by His hands! Is this not the carpenter, the Son of Mary, and brother of James, Joses, Judas, and Simon? And are not His sisters here with us?" So they were offended at Him. But Jesus said to them, "A prophet is not without honor except in his own country, among his own relatives, and in his own house." Now He could do no mighty work there, except that He laid His hands on a few sick people and healed* THEM. *And He marveled because of their unbelief. Then He went about the villages in a circuit, teaching.*

First notice a very important restraint that people put on the gifts of ministry that God has placed in our midst. They acknowledged His good works but discounted their value by seeing and judging Jesus after the flesh and not after the Spirit. When they start questioning not what He did but who He was in the flesh – that He is merely the "carpenter's son," what they are saying is that who does he think he is – he is just one of us. Many gifted men in the church are often judged by their background, heritage, scholarly credentials, or their human shortcoming, and the like, so that other people can discount what they do and therefore discount their God given authority.

It has also been little understood that we can in fact keep Jesus from doing things in our midst! There are good things He is WILLING TO DO that He won't do because we will not let Him. You see the prayer that "thy will be done on earth as it is in heaven" has new meaning in this context. His will happens every moment in heaven. There is "oneness" in heaven that generates fulfillment of His will without discussion.

<u>Matt 18:18-20</u> *"Assuredly, I say to you, whatever you bind on earth will be bound in heaven, and whatever you loose on earth will be loosed in heaven. "Again I say to you that if two of you agree on earth concerning anything that they ask, it will be done for them by My Father in heaven. For where two or three are gathered together in My name, I am there in the midst of them."*

On earth Jesus must find agreement! If two or more of you will agree on earth as touching anything it shall be done for them of my Father. The point here is that when those on earth find His will, agree together what that will is, and pray in faith believing that it is His will – and it is – it will be done on earth.

We often have tried to talk our way into this from many directions. For example, it's our will and we want to make it His will. Or we hope it is His will and we try to talk Him into it. Years ago there was a man who used the expression "you know in your knower!" That says it all. There is a place when "you know" that it is His will. You don't have to conjure up the energy or the faith to believe. You just know and believe. And when that same knowledge comes to two or more people then when they come together and express that faith in prayer it will happen.

Often in the degree of the request and the timing of that will by God – circumstances can seem to present roadblocks to fulfillment. But often the seeming delay is the working out of a confluence of events by God because of the interrelationship of His will for us and others at the same time.

For example, Moses thought he was called to be the leader of the children of Israel out of Egypt and into the Promised Land. We know that he was called for this task. But when Moses thought the time was right – it wasn't. God was waiting also for the hearts of the people to turn toward Him and desire Him to take them out of Egypt and to the Land promised to Abraham, Isaac, and Jacob.

From the time Moses thought he was ready to go and the children were actually ready to go was 40 years difference. Timing is often the key mystery to the equation in perceiving and experiencing the will of God. Humanly we don't handle time very well. Just like Moses did, we can give up on that "will" we thought we knew was from God

Peter in his journey was coming along in his faith in the expressed Power of God. By Jesus keeping him and the others with Him during the resurrection prayer it was a sign to us that Peter was not only in agreement but also believed she would rise from the dead. We see later that Peter himself in his ministry on earth likewise raised the dead to life.

Notice that Jesus removed those He knew were not in agreement from this resurrection event. This is a powerful truth that needs our application in the here and now. The more far reaching and life changing the will of God seems, the fewer should know about it. The "nay Sayers" evidently can compromise the agreement of a few.

The will of God on earth needs to find agreement between two or three to be accomplished. This is His rule and way for things to get done on earth. If we stop and consider how most things are done in the church, we see that the church on the local level often misses out on living and doing the will of God! Why? Because in our western culture we think we all have a voice in what is going to be done in our local assembly. We claim a "right to our opinion" that in fact is just that – an opinion. We evaluate spiritual decisions again with the 5 senses basing our opinion on what looks right, or feels right, or smells right, sounds right, or what tastes right. Since the things of the Spirit on are another plane, this application of our senses to make a judgment – makes no sense!

Then we have those situations where part of the group "acquiesces" and this is just as bad. They sit back to watch the group decision or the leader's decision fail. Then comes the flood of "I told you so" attacking every perceived shortcoming.

God's will is discerned in the "spirit." And we must start finding the keys to the Power of Agreement in the local church. This is where faith to move mountains comes from.

Another thought to add here is that the Will of God is not withheld from us. It is God's desire that we know his will and that we walk in it. When we come to those junctions is life as to whether we go this way or that way, it is his desire to show us the way. This is where faith comes into the equation. When we pray if faith believing that his will is revealed to us we will find out that it is.

Outline Chapter Five
Peter Participates in the Power of Agreement

1) Why did Jesus get rid of so many before He prayed?

2) Why doesn't faith in some overcome doubt in others?

3) As a believer can I make things happen?

4) What role does timing have in our prayers of faith?

5) What does this passage in Ezekiel tell us about influence on God by people?

Ezek 14:13,14 *"Son of man, when a land sins against Me by persistent unfaithfulness, I will stretch out My hand against it; I will cut off its supply of bread, send famine on it, and cut off man and beast from it. Even* IF *these three men, Noah, Daniel, and Job, were in it, they would deliver* ONLY *themselves by their righteousness," says the Lord GOD.*

CHAPTER SIX
THE LEGEND OF THE
TRANSFIGURATION:

<u>Luke 9:28–36</u> *Now it came to pass, about eight days after these sayings, that He took Peter, John, and James and went up on the mountain to pray. As He prayed, the appearance of His face was altered, and His robe* BECAME *white* AND *glistening. And behold, two men talked with Him, who were Moses and Elijah, who appeared in glory and spoke of His decease which He was about to accomplish at Jerusalem.*

But Peter and those with him were heavy with sleep; and when they were fully awake, they saw His glory and the two men who stood with Him. Then it happened, as they were parting from Him, THAT *Peter said to Jesus, "Master, it is good for us to be here; and let us make three tabernacles: one for You, one for Moses, and one for Elijah"—not knowing what he said. While he was saying this, a cloud came and overshadowed them; and they were fearful as they entered the cloud.*

And a voice came out of the cloud, saying, "This is My beloved Son. Hear Him!" When the voice had ceased, Jesus was found alone. But they kept quiet, and told no one in those days any of the things they had seen.

The transfiguration is not about Peter. Many a sermon has again mocked Peter over his reaction to an encounter with heaven on earth – and we have completely missed the point of the event.

Peter and the other two were to be witnesses to this event. This event was vital to the life of Jesus on earth and God the Father wanted it recorded for the church age. Again, this was a gathering of people in agreement to be able to believe what was about to happen – and as we will see later, their presence was for the purpose to witness to the church for all ages that God said this to Jesus.

The end of the ministry on earth by Jesus in human form was fast approaching. The time of His sacrificial death was at hand. Jesus was in a struggle. The pressure He was bearing was beyond our comprehension. He was facing suffering, pain, and separation from His Father for the first and only time in eternity. While there was evidently willingness to obey there was a struggle within Him because it was not yet His will. There had never been before and there has never been since any question but that the will of the Father, Son, and Holy Spirit is One!

It is vital to life on earth to understand that it was the Father's decision to give all humanity a free will. That is that each person would have a choice to accept or reject their Creator and His will to be done on earth. We know in the Garden of Gethsemane that Jesus' prayer was not my will but thy will be done. It was not till He walked out of the Garden was He able to say – we are One again. It is my will as it is my Father's will.

<u>1 Peter 2:24</u> *who Himself bore our sins in His own body on the tree, that we, having died to sins, might live for righteousness— by whose stripes you were healed.*

The choice use of the words -"His own self" - tells us that He came into Oneness with the Father in that garden as angels ministered to Him. After all He went forward and suffered and died. He learned firsthand obedience- but more importantly it was realigning His own will One with the Father.

The reason for dwelling on the significance of this point is to find the ramifications to what has become known as the "Mount of Transfiguration." The Father watched and felt in the Son the battle in the human soul that the Son was living with. In other words, Jesus had poured out His Divinity into human form to be subject to the same limitations that you and I face as He came to live on earth. And the Father knew the pain in the soul of the man Jesus was right up to the breaking point. Since the promise is that none will ever be subject to more than they can handle, the Father was sending two great leaders from history to strengthen the heart of Jesus.

No where during His life on earth did He ever act like God. All things He said and did can be done by any of us! Did He not say "greater things than I do will you do?" In the context of these human limitations God was giving Him a heavenly encounter to embolden Him for the task at hand. Curiously the Father did not send Gabriel or Michael- or one of the angels to perform the task.

But He sent Moses and Elijah - the deliverer of the children of Israel from the clutches of Egypt and the prophet of confrontation who had been whirled up to heaven in a chariot of fire. It clearly says they talked to Him about His coming death. Each was uniquely qualified with a life message that each had lived.

Consider the revelation of the need for a substitute that Moses had one day in the wilderness:

Exodus 32:30-32 *Now it came to pass on the next day that Moses said to the people, "You have committed a great sin. So now I will go up to the LORD; perhaps I can make atonement for your sin." Then Moses returned to the LORD and said, "Oh, these people have committed a great sin, and have made for themselves a god of gold! Yet now, if You will forgive their sin— but if not, I pray, blot me out of Your book which You have written."*

Moses knew the people were incapable of living right before God on their own. He also knew that God could require whatever He wanted from these people at this time. Right then and there in history came the revelation to a man that humankind needed a substitute. Moses offered himself, but he was not qualified to be the substitute.

But, Moses was qualified to minister to Jesus – urging Him on to the cross. The cross was the only solution acceptable to God. God had turned down the substitution of Moses. But now Moses knew that Jesus had passed the test, Jesus was qualified, and His sacrifice would be acceptable.

Elijah had his own qualifications.

1 Kings 18:22-29 *Then Elijah said to the people, "I alone am left a prophet of the LORD; but Baal's prophets ARE four hundred and fifty men. Therefore let them give us two bulls; and let them choose one bull for themselves, cut it in pieces, and lay IT on the wood, but put no fire UNDER IT; and I will prepare*

the other bull, and lay IT *on the wood, but put no fire* UNDER IT. *Then you call on the name of your gods, and I will call on the name of the LORD; and the God who answers by fire, He is God." So all the people answered and said, "It is well spoken." Now Elijah said to the prophets of Baal, "Choose one bull for yourselves and prepare* IT *first, for you* ARE *many; and call on the name of your god, but put no fire* UNDER IT.*"*

So they took the bull which was given them, and they prepared IT, *and called on the name of Baal from morning even till noon, saying, "O Baal, hear us!" But* THERE WAS *no voice; no one answered. Then they leaped about the altar which they had made. And so it was, at noon, that Elijah mocked them and said, "Cry aloud, for he* IS *a god; either he is meditating, or he is busy, or he is on a journey,* OR *perhaps he is sleeping and must be awakened."*

So they cried aloud, and cut themselves, as was their custom, with knives and lances, until the blood gushed out on them. And when midday was past, they prophesied until the TIME *of the offering of the* EVENING *sacrifice. But* THERE WAS *no voice; no one answered, no one paid attention.*

The story continues a few verses later:

<u>1 Kings 18: 36-39</u> *And it came to pass, at* THE TIME OF *the offering of the* EVENING *sacrifice, that Elijah the prophet came near and said, "LORD God of Abraham, Isaac, and Israel, let it be known this day that You* ARE *God in Israel and I* AM *Your servant, and* THAT *I have done all these things at Your word. Hear me, O LORD, hear me, that this people may know that You* ARE *the LORD God, and* THAT *You have*

turned their hearts back TO YOU *again." Then the fire of the LORD fell and consumed the burnt sacrifice, and the wood and the stones and the dust, and it licked up the water that* WAS *in the trench. Now when all the people saw* IT, *they fell on their faces; and they said, "The LORD, He* IS *God! The LORD, He* IS *God!"*

Elijah, in one of the most confrontational events between a man and the devil recorded in scripture- challenged the devil and his human minions to proof of power. The devil was defeated soundly, he couldn't talk and he couldn't bring fire as God did at the prayer request of Elijah. Jesus was certainly feeling the pressure of sin coming at Him.

He also had the devil whispering in His ear I am sure of how the cross was going to be a defeat not a victory. The devil is a liar. And Elijah no doubt declared if God the Father would answer my prayer You can rest assured He will answer yours!

We can be sure they were encouraging Him and reinforcing Him in the necessity and value of the sacrifice. They were also giving Him encouragement that the Father would protect Him at the moment of death. At death's door each of them knew that God's guiding hand would protect Jesus and most assuredly they were telling Jesus everything was in good hands.

Moses had offered to God to be blotted out of the book of Life for the sake of the people so he had a clear message of encouragement and understanding of the need of mankind for the act of substitution to bring salvation. Elijah had the message of confronting the devil at his own game. While the discussion took place there was an infusion in Jesus from heaven. The glow of the love of the Father came all over Him similar to the glow that was upon Moses coming down from the mount after 40 days and nights of fasting and fellowship with the Father.

Evidently the greater the task required by the Father the greater the support and love of the Father is demonstrated. "This is my beloved Son hear Him!" Are profound words **for Jesus!** Peter, James, and John were there to witness the event. The event though was for the encouragement and strengthening of Jesus.

In other words, the Father is saying that He trusts Jesus to carry through and He believes Jesus will fulfill all that is required for the sake of human kind. Let us remember Jesus could have "pulled the plug" any time He wanted to and all would be lost. Later He said He could call 12 legions – 72,000 angels – to come and stop the arrest and sentence to death.

The story has nothing to do with belittling the fact that Peter "wanted tabernacles to be built to commemorate the event." Peter did grasp that there was something profound in the encounter – but his role was as a witness not monument builder. This event required a witness to enable mankind of the church age to grasp the significance and the power of the sacrifice. Let no one belittle the forces at work for and against their salvation.

The battle was not for numbers or soldiers or swords – but the battle was for hearts. And the heart being ministered to and strengthened here is the heart of Jesus Himself! Let's take another moment to consider the context. Jesus was coming to His impending death. This moment had been known about and anticipated since sometime before the foundation of the world.

The clock was ticking – getting ready for the Big Game – is nothing compared to this. It is more like One Man going out to the battle field against 10,000 and thousands of thousands of foes. The stakes were the highest ever fought over. Jesus was facing this alone – and remember; He did it as a man, with all of our limitations. The prize was the souls of believers throughout the ages.

As the day draws closer the pressure is mounting. Certainly on the edges of His awareness, doubt was lurking. Do I really want to do this? After all, we can start this thing all over again if I don't! We have no place of reference to understanding the magnitude of the pressure. We can't imagine with our last breath saying, "I commend to you my spirit." Meaning, I give up control of that which I have always – through all of eternity-had control over- life itself. Consider the power of the love of God in this equation, "For God so loved the world that He sent His only begotten Son to die for us."

The will of God was that the Man Christ Jesus must die for you and me. Jesus knew it, and yet even later asked if there is an alternative let the alternative happen. Just as important to the present state of mind for Jesus at the Mount of Transfiguration, was the forward looking to the future.

Jesus looks around and sees the future church in the hands of a rather rag tag core group of about 120 people. He had 12 disciples, one of which was a traitor. He had a bunch of women, who in that culture and at the time had limited influence. Things looked tenuous to say the least. He needed an infusion of hope and faith from heaven and He got it! It is amazing when a few words of encouragement and a few words of the love of the Father can embolden us to accomplish the will of God on earth.

Thirty five to forty years later Peter recalled the event:

2 Peter 1:16-18 *For we did not follow cunningly devised fables when we made known to you the power and coming of our Lord Jesus Christ, but were eyewitnesses of His majesty. For He received from God the Father honor and glory when such a voice came to Him from the Excellent Glory: "This is My beloved Son, in whom I am well pleased." And we heard this voice which came from heaven when we were with Him on the holy mountain.*

While the "transfiguration" was vital to keep Jesus on track, it was also vital to the three witnesses to help verify that heaven was behind the Man they followed. We must take note that we are not expected to blindly follow Jesus like we do when we follow the latest fad that will give us mental health or lose weight or make us successful.

Jesus actually passes any legal test or for that matter scientific test. On the "Holy Mount" Jesus had 3 witnesses from among the disciples. The legal test is confirmation in the mouths of 2 or 3 witnesses. After His resurrection He was physically seen on at least 3 occasions by the 11 disciples, the other 109 that followed closely, and 500 on at least one of those times.

How do we know these disciples actually did see these things? Each of them lived for Him the rest of their days, and all gave their lives for him to the death! None walked away – none gave up – all preached to their dying day. Jesus and Christianity is not some fable or fad.

Outline Chapter Six
The Legend of the Transfiguration

1) Why do so many make fun of Peter for wanting to build booths for Jesus, Moses, and Elijah?

2) Why did God the Father call Jesus to come to the Mount?

3) How would you describe the struggle Jesus was having?

4) What was Jesus struggling with?

5) Was the "will of Jesus the man" now in line with the will of the Father?

CHAPTER SEVEN
INTRODUCTION TO
POLITICS AND RELIGION

<u>Matt 17:24-27</u> *When they had come to Capernaum, those who received the* TEMPLE *tax came to Peter and said, "Does your Teacher not pay the* TEMPLE *tax?" He said, "Yes." And when he had come into the house, Jesus anticipated him, saying, "What do you think, Simon? From whom do the kings of the earth take customs or taxes, from their sons or from strangers?"*

Peter said to Him, "From strangers." Jesus said to him, "Then the sons are free. Nevertheless, lest we offend them, go to the sea, cast in a hook, and take the fish that comes up first. And when you have opened its mouth, you will find a piece of money; take that and give it to them for Me and you."

How the church interacts with the society/culture it has found itself in has been a source of constant debate throughout history. Of course the church has grown in every culture on earth. In 1949 Mao imposed Communism on China and the church was "outlawed." In 1979 the power of Mao was over and Communism's strangle hold on Christianity was loosened somewhat. But what we found was that in 1949 there were about one million Christians in China and in 1979 there were estimates that there were 50 million Christians.

So regardless of the political climate the church will grow. Often growing quicker the more persecution it has to endure.

The relationship and responsibility of the "Church" to its culture has taken on many forms and has been cause for much debate. To gain some insight let's consider this analogy.

Every discipline has its own language. In science for example, there are accepted methods for proving theories. There are testing techniques, and measurements for cause and effect that rule this "world of science." In American football likewise there is language and rules that rule the "world of football." If you told a 230 lb. tail back to run through the lab and knock over all the lab techs it would be a pretty ridiculous scenario.

In the politics of any country – but let's focus on the USA – there is a language and rules that govern "the world of politics." Participation by all citizens in America is welcome but the degree of influence depends on the powers that be within the "particular party." In addition, money is a source of big influence. The power to influence voters to vote a certain way in a democracy is a great source of gaining power and position. As a result, decisions are usually made that will gain votes and not necessarily be what is in the best interests of all or what is for the common good.

Generally the church has had a declining impact in our democracy over the last 75 years. In the early years of our democracy our leaders unashamedly proclaimed the influence of the Bible upon their thinking and decision making. But this influence has had less and less appeal and less vote getting power as the Nation as a whole moves farther away from the Biblical principles of God.

<u>Acts 1:6-8</u> *Therefore, when they had come together, they asked Him, saying, "Lord, will You at this time restore the kingdom to Israel?" And He said to them, "It is not for you to know times or seasons which the Father has put in His own authority. But you shall receive power when the Holy Spirit has come upon you; and you shall be witnesses to Me in Jerusalem, and in all Judea and Samaria, and to the end of the earth."*

Right after the resurrection the disciples engaged Jesus in the discussion regarding the timing of the Kingdom of God being in power on earth. The disciples wanted to know whether Jesus was going to set up the Kingdom here and now. He said no. The day will come on His return that He will set up the Kingdom here on earth in Jerusalem and rule the world for a time. But that time is not now. And when it comes we will not make it come – it will happen when the Father says it will happen. Note though that Jesus said you will receive power in the here and now. It will be sourced through the Holy Spirit, but you are to use the power to witness to the saving grace of the resurrected Christ.

This then is our primary responsibility while we wait on the Father to set up the Kingdom. Regardless of politics we are to be His witnesses.

In our first text of this chapter (Matt 17: 24-27) Jesus is telling Peter let's pay taxes and not offend the political powers that be. We could say He was saying, let's not cause trouble, and let's be good citizens. Of course it would be nice if we could catch a fish to pay our taxes but that is not the point. The Bible is clear – we are to pay tribute where tribute is due. We are to pay honor where honor is due. We are to pray for those in authority including all political authority as noted below.

<u>1 Tim 2:1-3</u> *Therefore I exhort first of all that supplications, prayers, intercessions,* AND *giving of thanks be made for all men, for kings and all who are in authority, that we may lead a quiet and peaceable life in all godliness and reverence. For this* IS *good and acceptable in the sight of God our Savior,*

As an American we should vote and participate in the political process, serving locally or nationally as God would lead us. But we must remember we are fundamentally here to make ourselves eligible for use in the Kingdom of God. We are here to be a witness for Him. We are here to make disciples teaching others to live for Christ. And when we are "called or lead" to be in the "world of politics" that the rules and language are different and we can't just "run through the lab knocking people over."

I have found by experience that when Christians work in the political arena it can be like the tail back running through the lab. I have watched them try to "impose" what they claim is the will of God and it completely turns off the others in politics and the electorate. Many Christians walk around in presumption and this manner does not work in the world of politics.

The rules of engagement are completely different. The decision making process is not based on what is best for all. At every level decisions are made to advance particular groups, particular geographic areas, and particular personal agendas- and above all it is to get votes to advance some agreed to agenda. It is not trying to discern what God wants done. Therefore conflict is certain for Christians and the competitive rules get down and dirty when it comes to advancing any cause or election.

This is not to say Christians must avoid politics altogether. Our witness needs to pervade the society. But we are not here to convert the institutions of society; we are here to convert the people of our society. We do need the Daniels and the Esther's of this world to be in the right place at the right time for the will of God to be implemented. Surely they need to be harmless as doves and wise as serpents.

Usually it happens that the Christian in politics is very naïve. For an exception if we look at the life of a politician like Wilberforce in England in the early 1800's we find a man on a mission to stop slave trading that took about 30 years to get through the House of Parliament. No one disagreed with the inhumanity of it all, but there was big money that demanded it keep going. It was only when the French were using the American flag to sail under with slaves on board, and the British were at war with the French did Wilberforce find a way to stop slave trading using that method. In the world of politics just because "it is the right thing to do," does not mean it will get done.

Many vocal Christian leaders in the 1970's called the church to political action. Millions of dollars were raised and hundreds of meetings were held to rally people to action. Unfortunately, as we look back we see the results were short lived at best. We found a sincere Christian man named Jimmy Carter represented only one narrow view of Christianity and many Christians – for political reasons – were opposed to that view. Other proclaiming Christians subsequently came into the White House that also disappointed many segments of the Church and the Church found out political consensus is virtually impossible to achieve in the Church let alone in the society at large.

This is because politics has its own language and its own rules of engagement that are often opposed to what the Church would say represented a Christian World View.

Outline Chapter Seven
Introduction to Politics and Religion

1) Did Jesus ever complain about the Roman rule in Israel?

2) So even occupiers and a two tiered tax system (Rome and the Synagogue) were not fought against by Jesus?

3) Why is the influence of the gospel diminishing in American politics?

4) How can Christians influence the world of politics?

CHAPTER EIGHT
INSIGHT AND
INTRODUCTION TO
CHRISTIAN
RELATIONSHIPS

<u>Matt 18:21-35</u>   *Then Peter came to Him and said, "Lord, how often shall my brother sin against me, and I forgive him? Up to seven times?" Jesus said to him, "I do not say to you, up to seven times, but up to seventy times seven. Therefore the kingdom of heaven is like a certain king who wanted to settle accounts with his servants.*

And when he had begun to settle accounts, one was brought to him who owed him ten thousand talents. But as he was not able to pay, his master commanded that he be sold, with his wife and children and all that he had, and that payment be made. The servant therefore fell down before him, saying, 'Master, have patience with me, and I will pay you all.' Then the master of that servant was moved with compassion, released him, and forgave him the debt.

"But that servant went out and found one of his fellow servants who owed him a hundred denarii; and he laid hands on him and took HIM by the throat, saying, 'Pay me what you owe!' So his fellow servant fell down at his feet and begged him, saying, 'Have patience with me, and I will pay you all.' And he would

not, but went and threw him into prison till he should pay the debt. So when his fellow servants saw what had been done, they were very grieved, and came and told their master all that had been done. Then his master, after he had called him, said to him,

'You wicked servant! I forgave you all that debt because you begged me. Should you not also have had compassion on your fellow servant, just as I had pity on you?' And his master was angry, and delivered him to the torturers until he should pay all that was due to him. "So My heavenly Father also will do to you if each of you, from his heart, does not forgive his brother his trespasses."

In order to build a context for our human minds to grasp the significance of this revelation we must take into consideration the human condition. There is a Creator God who has created all human beings and therefore we have an obligation to our Creator. That obligation is very simple and yet over whelming. We are intended to be holy as He is Holy. We are to be pure as He is pure. We are to be perfect as He is perfect. Yet every one of us ever born on the planet has fallen short of this legitimate demand.

Because ALL have sinned and fallen short of the glory of God the result is that this failure creates a debt or obligation that each of us owes to our Creator. Every sin requires payment for failure. This debt is virtually insurmountable for us to "pay back." Think of yourself as having a net worth of $100 and an income of $1 per week. But that you owe someone one billion trillion dollars.

In other words it is totally impossible for you and me to ever pay it back. So this Creator God – who is also a loving God – has seen our dilemma and has come up with a solution. What will pay for our sins is the sacrificial blood of His Son being born on this earth just as Adam was, but him living a life of perfection in all purity and holiness, then Him dying on the cross, and then rising from the dead by the Holy Spirit. His resurrection is our proof that His shed blood was sufficient to pay for our sins. There is no amount of money and no amount of good works that anyone could ever do to make up the deficit any other way.

The Good News is no one will go to hell because of their sins. Hell is only for the devil and his angels and unfortunately now also for those who refuse to believe that the payment of the death of Christ was sufficient payment for their sins.

As a result of the death and sacrifice of Jesus for my sins I now owe God everything. In other words before His death and resurrection I owed him a debt I could never pay. After I accept His payment on my behalf I now owe Him my very soul. I am bought and paid for. The thing about His ownership of me that makes this a joy is that He is a beneficial owner that has my best interests at heart. His ownership means life and before I had placed myself under that ownership I was doomed to death. His ownership means healing and joy and prosperity. But when I was under my untenable obligation my life meant sickness death and destruction. It is a good thing to be under His tutelage and ownership.

It is also very important to understand something about the debt we all originally owed to God prior to accepting His method of provision of payment. He could take no markdowns for what we owed. He could not write it off, He could not discount in anyway the obligation that every human being owed.

Now when we have understanding of this context it is worth reading the above passage again.

Forgiveness is a fundamental principle of the Kingdom of God while we are in the present Church age. We forgive each other because He forgave us. The whole topic of forgiveness begins with understanding the power and benefits of forgiveness that we as believers enjoy. Forgiveness means to send away. The Bible says that God sends our sins away as far as the east is from the west (infinity). It says that God will no more remember our shortcomings or failures of sin.

As a result of this benefit of being a believer it then places an obligation on interpersonal relationships among fellow believers. Since we have in common the benefit that all of our sins have been forgiven we therefore must practice forgiveness within our community of believers.

Anything we receive from God is not just for our own use but is to be a common practice as we live and move on this earth. It goes without saying that believers continue to make mistakes. We surly already know by experience that we will commit acts against one another that will hurt or offend one another. The principle of forgiveness lays down the law of liberty in the New Testament in how to deal with all offences against us.

Matt 6:10-15 Our Father in heaven, Hallowed be Your name. Your kingdom come. Your will be done On earth as IT IS in heaven. Give us this day our daily bread. And forgive us our debts, As we forgive our debtors. And do not lead us into temptation, But deliver us from the evil one. For Yours is the kingdom and the power and the glory forever. Amen. "For if you forgive men their trespasses, your heavenly Father will also forgive you. But if you do not forgive men their trespasses, neither will your Father forgive your trespasses.

Mark 11:25 And when ye stand praying, forgive, if ye have ought against any: that your Father also which is in heaven may forgive you your trespasses.

Mark 11:26 But if ye do not forgive, neither will your Father which is in heaven forgive your trespasses.

In the course of human endeavors as people walk side by side working together or living together each will do those things that the other will not like or perceive that are against them. Conflict arises over how to achieve agreement in the process of sharing life together. In its simplest form one thinks it is better to do it this way and the other thinks it's better to do it that way.

There are those that want to do it their way regardless. Conflict also arises when one tries to dominate every time how things are done or what is done. In working or living together with someone it requires give and take as a part of this relationship. Harmony can be difficult to find and compromise inevitably must come into play.

In a typical situation we find one person offending another has created an obligation from the offender to the offended. But when the offended person makes a choice to "send away" the obligation, without requiring any payment for this obligation, this is forgiveness

When you have a personality like Peter, we can assume he was driven by obsessive compulsive tendencies, and that he would be one that would keep pushing to get his own way regardless. He was probably constantly "mad or at least aggravated" at his fellow disciples for not seeing things his way – or at the least they were aggravated at him for always pushing. Evidently there were regular arguments over who were the leaders among the disciples. The question to Jesus by Peter in our text was not out of the blue! In this text it seems clear that he was asking Jesus, "How many times do I have to forgive these guys?"

Jesus mercifully teaches by analogy to put the understanding of forgiveness into perspective. Obviously, first and foremost we are all sinners. All have sinned and come short of the glory of God. Therefore, a fundamental requirement of any relationship with God requires that we "find" the way to gain His forgiveness. He provided that way through the sacrifice of His Son on our behalf. And our acceptance and belief that His Son's sacrifice paid for our shortcomings enables us to ask for and receive His forgiveness for our failings and shortcomings.

Therefore because we have been forgiven we must forgive. We cannot fully receive forgiveness if we do not also have the ability to forgive others. In other words, if we understand we are forgiven we will forgive. When we see and know and experience forgiveness it will be a part of our life attitude toward others. As we experience forgiveness we will extend that which we experience.

One time a man said to me how do you get love? I told him you give it to others then it will come to you. When I am given love I will give love. When I am given peace I will give peace to others. Jesus gives us the bread of life – not just for our own consumption, but that we might have to give to others. Our life in Christ is all about being a vessel. We don't consume the things of God we receive from Him all on ourselves. But we receive from Him a sufficiency and have enough for ourselves and enough to give the things of God to others. We find his principles are based on a paradigm of multiplication. In other words, what He gives us we give to others and in fact end up getting more for ourselves.

This is borne out by the principle of sowing and reaping. It applies to all aspects of life in Christ. As we plant in others we will reap for ourselves. We will reap sufficient to plant some more, have more for ourselves, and also have for others. The more you "plant" or sow the more you reap and the more you have to further use, plant, and reap. This is the principle of abundant living.

Gal 5:22 But the fruit of the Spirit is love, joy, peace, longsuffering, gentleness, goodness, faith,

In other words, the evidence of God in our lives is marked by our living in the expression of the fruit of His relationship being a part of our everyday living. Therefore forgiveness will flow out of the heart of the believer and when it does not the believer is probably struggling with trying to understand that he has been forgiven.

It is a wonder to me that all humans in every society have a sense of failure. They all know that they have done wrong and they all have a need to "do something to make up for the wrong they have done." They know they have fallen short even if they do not understand who it is that they fell short of. Anything from animal sacrifices, to personal sacrifice or even personal disfigurement on some level is virtually a part of every society. People have an innate need to pay for or make up for their failures.

We learn in the New Testament that animal sacrifice in the Old Testament only "covered" the sins of those who did it. One day when John the Baptist was water baptizing he looked up and saw Jesus and proclaimed, "Behold, the Lamb of God that TAKES AWAY the sins of the world." Yes, a sacrifice was coming into play but the Lamb was not a 4 legged creature without blemish. The Lamb was in fact the One who is the King of the World.

Forgiveness of sin is the biggest benefit to the Kingdom of God on earth. Imagine the fact that not only can I not pay for my own sins – no matter the degree or seriousness of the sin – but that by His grace I can receive forgiveness immediately. Forgiveness is an important principle in the Kingdom here on earth. Love is the primary currency but forgiveness is evidence that that love is real. It is to be what believers should be giving and receiving to one another along life's way.

When the disciples were preparing to participate in the Last Supper, Jesus as we know stripped down and took a bowl and cloth and then went around the table to wash the feet of each disciple. It was a profound event because up until this time there were constant arguments among the disciples of who would take over the leadership of the group. They were starting to anticipate the coming Kingdom and were fighting for position as it were. Jesus needed to deal with this now at the eleventh hour of His time on earth so that the church could at least start off without people fighting for position.

<u>John 13:3-10</u> *Jesus, knowing that the Father had given all things into His hands, and that He had come from God and was going to God, rose from supper and laid aside His garments, took a towel and girded Himself. After that, He poured water into a basin and began to wash the disciples' feet, and to wipe* THEM *with the towel with which He was girded. Then He came to Simon Peter. And* PETER *said to Him, "Lord, are You washing my feet?" Jesus answered and said to him, "What I am doing you do not understand now, but you will know after this." Peter said to Him, "You shall never wash my feet!" Jesus answered him, "If I do not wash you, you have no part with Me." Simon Peter said to Him, "Lord, not my feet only, but also* MY *hands and* MY *head!" Jesus said to him, "He who is bathed needs only to wash* HIS *feet, but is completely clean; and you are clean, but not all of you."*

Jesus put an end to the arguments by humbling himself as an example for how the Kingdom works. Whoever would be "chief" would first of all be required to be a servant. Jesus constantly was giving the paradigm of the Kingdom. Love –

forgive – serve – humility – sacrifice – are key words for expressing the success of the Kingdom. You don't fight to get ahead, you don't knock down others, and you don't outsmart others. But rather you strive toward holiness, living in purity, responding to the direction of the Holy Spirit and let the Father promote into leadership those He chooses.

When we "wrong" someone, whether in word or action, it somehow even obligates us in our own heart. Depending on the severity, we feel we must "make up for it" somehow or some way. Of course, there are those who have wronged so many that their heart becomes harden to the fact that some type obligation is there. These are poor lost souls who have a deep sense of guilt but cannot find their own forgiveness from God and therefore are unable and unwilling to give forgiveness to others.

To be forgiven is to be set free. When we are free in relationship to one another we are then free to come into agreement – and you know what happens then! We have the power to impose the will of God on earth. Interestingly the Koran is quite silent on forgiveness among men. They teach about forgiveness of Allah, but that forgiveness among men is a sign of weakness. In reality, forgiveness is a power. When I follow the Biblical admonition to forgive my enemies and do good to those that harm me, in reality, it shows the power of God at work in my heart and life.

It has been said that 85% of all those who have come to the saving knowledge of Jesus Christ as their Savior have done so by the time they are 18 years of age. It seems that the longer we practice sin and harbor unforgiveness toward others, the "harder" our heart becomes. The longer we live without forgiveness ourselves the longer and harder it is for us to forgive. The church needs a new urgency in reaching the lost while they are still young. The older we get without forgiveness the harder it is to believe we can be forgiven.

If we follow this thinking and just look in the Bible for examples, we should come into the realization that children have the capacity to open their "spirit" to the saving grace of Jesus Christ. For some reason we think in the western church that we need to entertain them and just give them "little Bible stories." But if we look at Samuel, David, Shadrach, Meshach, and Abednego, Esther, Mary the mother of Jesus and many others we will see that great capacity to comprehend and fulfill the word of God in their lives at very early ages is possible.

In fact, the older people are when they come to the saving knowledge of Christ, the needier they are recovering from their past and their lifelong experiences of failure. This is usually based on the fact that there are multiple times people have wronged them and they had no means of resolution so they harbored those hurt and unforgiving feelings. In addition, they likewise hurt and harmed others along life's way so there is always a measure of guilt and hardness of heart hindering the soul of the unbeliever and making it very difficult for them to comprehend that the love of God is so powerful that it can wipe way all of life's hurts.

Outline Chapter Eight
Insight and Introduction to Christian
Relationships

1) What does forgiveness do to a relationship?

2) Why is it needed as a fundamental aspect of relationship?

3) If we have trouble forgiving others, what is this a sign of?

4) How does the principle of sowing and reaping apply to Christian relationships?

5) Why should there be a major shift to bringing "spiritual experiences" to children under 18 years of age.

CHAPTER NINE
ECONOMIC LESSON IN
THE KINGDOM OF GOD
ON EARTH:

<u>Matt 19:23-30</u> *Then Jesus said to His disciples, "Assuredly, I say to you that it is hard for a rich man to enter the kingdom of heaven. And again I say to you, it is easier for a camel to go through the eye of a needle than for a rich man to enter the kingdom of God."When His disciples heard* IT, *they were greatly astonished, saying, "Who then can be saved?"*

But Jesus looked at THEM *and said to them, "With men this is impossible, but with God all things are possible." Then Peter answered and said to Him, "See, we have left all and followed You. Therefore what shall we have?"*

So Jesus said to them, "Assuredly I say to you, that in the regeneration, when the Son of Man sits on the throne of His glory, you who have followed Me will also sit on twelve thrones, judging the twelve tribes of Israel. And everyone who has left houses or brothers or sisters or father or mother or wife or children or lands, for My name's sake, shall receive a hundredfold, and inherit eternal life. But many WHO ARE *first will be last, and the last first.*

Every group of people that have ever formed and lived together in any size community setting has quickly developed an economic aspect to their relationships with one another. Whether hunting or fishing up to manufacturing or creating values in service or technology there has evolved a value system to the work performed that rewards people on some level for their contribution.

Most societies along man's history have taken special note of the man who gained the most "riches" within any group. Historically we will find the rich man to be the most recognized, the most revered and usually the man who gets his way when he wants it.

So when Jesus says "it is hard for a rich man to come into the Kingdom of God" it again is contrary to human thinking and understanding. Throughout history the rich man had been able to "trust in his riches." He can get the exceptions to the rules done in his favor. He can buy and sell virtually whatever he wants including people, places, and things. He can have the women of his choice and indulge in the pleasures of his choice.

The rich man has a serious problem and does not know it. He does not know he needs forgiveness for his sins and they cannot be bought- by him. To tell a rich man that only Jesus can pay for them on his behalf absolutely does not make sense to him in the world view he naturally holds. What Jesus is saying here is that it is not that God is against rich men and doesn't want them in the Kingdom. But those rich men are against God in that they generally want God on their own terms like everything else in their life.

There is a curious turn in this account. While it is impossible for the rich man to come into the Kingdom – meaning on his own terms – Jesus at the same time says that even the impossible is possible with God. This means that God has a "way" for rich men to come into the knowledge of their need and find the way of forgiveness. Man left to his own devices can never find it but by the Spirit of God it is possible.

Then Peter asked a profound question of Jesus – since they were talking about economics. Peter said we left all we had – I gave up my boat, my nets, my dock and we are living with you; hand to mouth so to speak. We are not saving any money; we live off the offerings of the rich women of the household of Herod, and food given here and there. We don't know what's coming tomorrow and we don't know what is coming in our old age.

In other words, Peter is asking how does the economics work in this journey we are on to bring forth your Kingdom. While we assume when your Kingdom is manifest things will be ok but in the mean time how does it work?

Jesus says a profound truth that has both present and future application. He says first, those who leave family, houses, friends, and means of support will receive a hundred fold return on their investment. In other words, whatever you left will be returned to you in this life here on earth in the here and now. Take no thought what you will wear or what you will eat. There is provision supplied.

In addition, in the world (Kingdom) to come the provision is there also – and it is forever. The concept of economics is strange in Kingdom thinking. Again the sowing and reaping principle applies. In the world, the economics of a society usually sets the rules of how the society operates. In the USA for example, there are hourly wages negotiated based on supply and demand for each job. We will not bother here with the variables involved suffice it to say values for contributions of work are determined in the "market place."

It seems from the teachings of Jesus that He addresses economics more than he does salvation in terms of actual content of teaching. Because He knows that economics usually drives the motivations and reasons for doing things in the world. You might say the fundamental principles of economics in most societies are based on keeping what you have and using it to make more.

However, in the Kingdom of God on earth economics are driven by giving. If we give we will receive. As usual the Kingdom thinking is opposite of world thinking.

Luke 6:36-38 *And if you do good to those who do good to you, what credit is that to you? For even sinners do the same. And if you lend* TO THOSE *from whom you hope to receive back, what credit is that to you? For even sinners lend to sinners to receive as much back. But love your enemies, do good, and lend, hoping for nothing in return; and your reward will be great, and you will be sons of the Most High.*

For He is kind to the unthankful and evil. Therefore be merciful, just as your Father also is merciful. "Judge not, and you shall not be judged. Condemn not, and you shall not be condemned. Forgive, and you will be forgiven. Give, and it will be given to you: good measure, pressed down, shaken together, and running over will be put into your bosom. For with the same measure that you use, it will be measured back to you."

So when Peter says we "gave all" to follow you Jesus says in answer – "great, and the reward will be profound, you will receive one hundred times what you have given – in this lifetime!" Not only that, but, as you will learn to live in the economics of the Kingdom you will find that again things work different from the world system.

In the world you are taught to do things for those that can or will as a result do things back for you. But in the economic system in God's Kingdom – the key is to do things for those that cannot do things back for you. In the world you are taught to lend to those who will pay back with interest, in God's Kingdom you lend to those that not only can't pay interest, but they cannot pay back what they owe you.

In the world you are taught to hate your enemies, in God's Kingdom you are told to love your enemies and to do good things for them without expectation of return. Be merciful, judge not, forgive, and give are all principles of the paradigm in Kingdom living here on earth.

So now we see the belief system of the Kingdom of God on earth is marked by key words that reveal the heart of the Father and are to become descriptions of our character and behavior here on earth. Now if we were to "Google" search for a Christian maybe these are more of the key words we should add that should bring us better results;

A heart after God's own heart - Love – forgive – serve – humility – sacrifice – lend without expectation – be merciful – love your enemies – don't judge others – give – do good

These words fly in the face of all other political and economic systems on earth. There are other religious groups that have some of these words to describe their behavior and attitudes but usually you will see that the sacrifices above are meant for the individual to do without. Most other religious thinking is that these types of attitudes and behaviors take away something from the adherent. But in Christianity these things add to us and our life experiences become more fulfilling. In God's economy it is intended that we do and act this way and at the same time we benefit not only psychologically but also spiritually and PHYSICALLY.

Yes, we are to deny ourselves and take up our "cross" (or burden) daily. But not so that we live our lives in misery but live our lives in fulfillment. While some are called to live in the jungles or in the Arctic's of the world to reach the lost-even in those conditions there are places of prosperity where harmony of soul – spirit – and body are possible.

I went to a place above the Arctic Circle near a city named Vorkuta. This city had been built by Stalin and was a place where the banished intelligentsia was sent in the late '30's. It was a coal mining town and today is forty six hours by train north of Moscow. It is twelve hours by train north of the nearest road. This city is surrounded by the Tundra. No trees grow and only grass like vegetation grows there. The Komi Tribe are the natives of this land and they "follow" deer herds and manage the herds. There are thirty five battalions in this tribe and over half of them have become Christians. Upon visiting them out on the Tundra I was amazed at their wealth. While living in a tent and it is fifty degrees below zero it might not sound like wealth to most Americans.

But they have everything they need and want. They VACATION two weeks to three weeks per year and rent apartments in the city of Vorkuta. They supply the city with meat, clothing, and warm deer skin boots. No cattle can live there so the city depends on deer to supply most of their needs. In America we seem to be losing the sense of adding value as a purpose in our work. We seem preoccupied with wanting or getting our wants and needs met – without thinking in terms of what we can provide to gain these things.

The Bible says: 2 Thess. 3:10 *For even when we were with you, we commanded you this: If anyone will not work, neither shall he eat.*

It is vital to remember there are promises not only for the life to come – but promises for this life as well. When our sacrifices seem only like loss then something is out of order. In the Kingdom of God on earth sacrifice will always seem like gain – because as you give you will also receive. In fact, as the end draws near the Bible says the "reaper will overtake the sower." This means that receiving will overtake giving, so that even before we are able to give in the situation we will start receiving as if we had already given.

Outline Chapter Nine
A Lesson in Economics in the Kingdom of God on Earth

1) Why would Jesus say that a rich man can't get into the Kingdom of God?

2) How does God provide the economic means for a rich man to enter the Kingdom?

3) Why would Peter want to know the economic benefits of being a disciple?

4) Describe the economics that Jesus proposes that rule the Kingdom.

5) How important are economics when the nature of the Kingdom is spiritually based?

CHAPTER TEN
PETER FOREWARNED HE WOULD FAIL- PART 1

<u>Luke 22:31-34</u> *And the Lord said, "Simon, Simon! Indeed, Satan has asked for you, that he may sift* YOU *as wheat. But I have prayed for you, that your faith should not fail; and when you have returned to* ME, *strengthen your brethren." But he said to Him, "Lord, I am ready to go with You, both to prison and to death." Then He said, "I tell you, Peter, the rooster shall not crow this day before you will deny three times that you know Me."*

<u>John 13:34-38</u> *A new commandment I give to you, that you love one another; as I have loved you, that you also love one another. By this all will know that you are My disciples, if you have love for one another."Jesus Predicts Peter's Denial Simon Peter said to Him, "Lord, where are You going?"Jesus answered him, "Where I am going you cannot follow Me now, but you shall follow Me afterward." Peter said to Him, "Lord, why can I not follow You now? I will lay down my life for Your sake." Jesus answered him, "Will you lay down your life for My sake? Most assuredly, I say to you, the rooster shall not crow till you have denied Me three times.*

This event is broken into two parts to enable us to grasp two lessons on Peter's journey to find LIFE. A constantly asked question in the Christian life throughout history has been - why did this or that happen to me? Why did I have to go through all the things I went through? Why did not God spare me of the troubles I've seen? Again the paradigm of the Kingdom usually works the opposite of our human rationale. First of all let us be aware there is an enemy out there on the loose. Too often we are attributing to God what is actually being engineered and manipulated by Satan.

Evidently Satan had been around God appealing to God to lift the "hedge up" from around Peter – just like he did with Job – and let Satan get at him. I can hear Satan now saying Peter only serves Jesus now because he wants to be the ruler of the church. Let me at him and I will show you he is a phony and that Your plan will not work.

Job 1:6-12 *Now there was a day when the sons of God came to present themselves before the LORD, and Satan also came among them. And the LORD said to Satan, "From where do you come?"So Satan answered the LORD and said, "From going to and fro on the earth, and from walking back and forth on it." Then the LORD said to Satan, "Have you considered My servant Job, that* THERE IS *none like him on the earth, a blameless and upright man, one who fears God and shuns evil?"*

So Satan answered the LORD and said, "Does Job fear God for nothing? Have You not made a hedge around him, around his household, and around all that he has on every side? You have blessed the work of his hands, and his possessions have increased in the land. But now, stretch out Your hand and touch all that he has, and he will surely curse You to Your face!"And the LORD said to Satan, "Behold, all that he has IS *in your power; only do not lay a hand on his* PERSON.*" So Satan went out from the presence of the LORD.*

It is very difficult for us to understand this kind of scenario or to even consider that these types of discussions even take place in heaven of all places. But remember God is not afraid of our enemy. Our enemy has certain restraints on him placed there by God. In addition, his actions are further limited by what WE ALLOW through our vulnerabilities. In the warning of Jesus – he clearly says to Peter "Satan desires to have you and sift you!" Notice the prayer of Jesus is for strength to Peter's faith that he will hold on to get through the experience and *not* for strength to avoid. This is important to understand the shade of meaning here. As we will see there was a great vulnerability in Peter that needed healing and this was at the foundation of the upcoming trial.

Now there is a lot going on in these connected passages. First, Jesus says in essence, Satan wants at you Peter, but I am praying your faith won't fail. THEN, (after you get through it Peter and you will get through it!), I want you to minister your victory of getting through to others. This means that it will be a common experience in the life of the church that many will fail in their commitments. And this failure will need to be dealt with in such a way to heal the person and keep the failure from destroying the person who fails.

Now many will ask, "Why did not Jesus merely bind up Satan and not let him at Peter and just tell him what was wrong?"

James 1:12-15 *Blessed* IS *the man who endures temptation; for when he has been approved, he will receive the crown of life which the Lord has promised to those who love Him. Let no one say when he is tempted, "I am tempted by God"; for God cannot be tempted by evil, nor does He Himself tempt anyone. But each one is tempted when he is drawn away by his own desires and enticed. Then, when desire has conceived, it gives birth to sin; and sin, when it is full-grown, brings forth death.*

We already know that Peter had ambition. We also know his compulsive behavior and his quickness to speak out offering opinions at every turn. It is imperative to see here that Jesus did not want to spare Peter the test. It is from a test that we get a testimony. Jesus told Peter and we can therefore tell ourselves in our times of testing, that the key to any test is faith. Our faith CAN FAIL US. Jesus' foretelling prayer proclaimed that He prayed Peter's faith would not fail.

Peter had a key role to play in the birth of the church and this deep rooted heart issue or iniquity needed to be dealt with. Peter had not- up until now - been able to deal with the issue, and in fact was evidently unaware of the issue or its root cause in his own heart. There is a mercy from God that will provide means and methods of awareness of shortcomings or weaknesses in our own character that if left unchecked could be our downfall later on.

Whenever church leaders have "fallen" it has invariably been the result of an iniquity, or a root cause deep in their heart, that they missed opportunities to be aware of and deal with. Finally, their lust has conceived and brought forth sin. Notice Jesus did not argue with Peter's macho claim that he would follow him even unto death. That may have been Peter's emotional reaction to the pressure of the moment, but as events unfolded it would not be his actual reaction. After all Jesus did not want him to die anyway. Again while Peter was feeling that this was about him and it wasn't, it was about Jesus and the cup that He must drink.

There is an old adage "forewarned is forearmed." Jesus was letting Peter know that his good intentions would prove to not be real – and that Peter was going to face himself in the mirror as never before.

The church has often suffered the good intentions of people. I have heard people get caught up in the moment and declare this is the greatest church and I will stay here forever, only to not be seen after a week or two when something didn't go right as far as they were concerned. There is another old adage – "the road to hell is paved with good intentions." In Christianity, the only promises we can cling to are the Promises of God. The Promises of God will be fulfilled as we walk in the conditions of the Promise.

Peter had a streak in him that is needed for the kind of public ministry that Jesus had in mind for him as the church was about to be birthed. In this streak however, there was a tendency in Peter that would misuse the gift and Jesus needed to get his finger on it and get it dealt with before the resurrection.

We will see this in Part 2.

Outline Chapter Ten
Peter Forewarned He Would Fail
Part 1

---

1) Why would Jesus warn Peter about Satan?

2) Why not pray Satan would not be allowed to do it to Peter?

3) What had Peter promised Jesus?

4) Why did Peter not want Jesus to die?

5) Why did Satan have a "right" to go after Peter?

CHAPTER ELEVEN
PETER'S CONVERSION
PART 2

<u>Matt 26:64-75</u> *They answered and said, "He (Jesus) is deserving of death." Then they spat in His face and beat Him; and others struck* HIM *with the palms of their hands, saying, "Prophesy to us, Christ! Who is the one who struck You?" Now Peter sat outside in the courtyard. And a servant girl came to him, saying, "You also were with Jesus of Galilee." But* **he denied** *it before* THEM *all, saying, "I do not know what you are saying." And when he had gone out to the gateway, another* GIRL *saw him and said to those* WHO WERE *there, "This* FELLOW *also was with Jesus of Nazareth."*

But **again he denied** *with an oath, "I do not know the Man!" And a little later those who stood by came up and said to Peter, "Surely you also are* ONE *of them, for your speech betrays you." Then he began to curse and swear,* SAYING, **"I do not know the Man!"** *Immediately a rooster crowed. And Peter remembered the word of Jesus who had said to him, "Before the rooster crows, you will deny Me three times." So he went out and wept bitterly.*

It seems simple enough – Peter was a braggart, covetous and a liar. But it goes much deeper than that. Full of bravado in the confines of the upper room where friends shared a meal – but now out amongst the enemy with death and persecution in the air – reality and true issues of the heart are manifest.

Peter was a bitter man and when he "wept bitterly" his tears revealed the depth of his painful bitterness. Finally his secret bitterness came to the surface. He had never had to face it until now at the crucial time of the final trial of Jesus.

It was a moment of healing and deliverance for Peter; this was a moment that Jesus knew Peter must experience in order to be fully used in the birth of the church. Never again do you ever hear of unrealistic claims coming out of Peter. Oh, he was not yet perfect by any means; he still had issues coming to terms with the freedom in Christ and some of his religious upbringing that still kept him in bondage. But here the root cause of bitterness started to get dealt with so that he might have grace to open his arms to all that would come to the saving knowledge of Christ.

The bitter root that Jesus would allow Satan to reveal to Peter was something that flavored every aspect of the life of Peter. Peter was a bitter man. When Jesus had told Peter, "Get behind me Satan," He was telling Peter that there was something in Peter that kept rearing its ugly head and needed dealing with. But Peter never could or would acknowledge it.

Bitterness in a person blocks that person from gratitude and forbearance in dealing with others. A bitter person always wants more, is quick to judge the wrongs of others, and always feels others are against him. This was a serious root of iniquity and Satan was ready to exploit it to thwart the work of the Kingdom of God on earth.

A bitter person taints the group they are a part of. A bitter person is never satisfied. A bitter person is always the victim. The root of bitterness is just that, it permeates the words, thoughts and actions of the bitter person.

One might ask, "why didn't Jesus just talk to Peter and tell him to quit being bitter?" When it comes to dealing with deep seated issues like iniquity in the life of the person; we will find that there is a "stronghold" built around the flaw or shortcoming. It is a place in the heart of a person that has been defended and protected by the person all their life. In order for the stronghold to be broken, it takes a life changing confrontation where the person finally sees and admits it is there. It is almost as if the person has denied its existence so long that they cannot even see it themselves.

What is obvious to others is sometimes hard to come to grips with. Jesus let Satan come at Peter and prayed that as Peter finally came to face to face with his iniquity that his 3 lies or denials of Jesus would force Peter to see his iniquity – but that rather than use it as an excuse to run away from the call on his life, that it would be a time of healing and drawing Peter more solidly into the life Christ had planned for Peter. In order for this to be a positive experience for Peter he needed faith to trust God was with him even in his moment of exposure. Hence Jesus prayed that faith would rise up in Peter to see him through.

It was vital for the axe to cut off the root of bitterness in Peter. As a result of the mercy of God in using Peter's denial as a time to uproot the bitterness in the soul of Peter- we can look at the early ministry results in the book of Acts:

Acts 8:18-24 *And when Simon saw that through the laying on of the apostles' hands the Holy Spirit was given, he offered them money, saying, "Give me this power also, that anyone on whom I lay hands may receive the Holy Spirit." But Peter said to him, "Your money perish with you, because you thought that the gift of God could be purchased with money!*

You have neither part nor portion in this matter, for your heart is not right in the sight of God. Repent therefore of this your wickedness, and pray God if perhaps the thought of your heart may be forgiven you. For I see that you are poisoned by bitterness and bound by iniquity." Then Simon answered and said, "Pray to the Lord for me, that none of the things which you have spoken may come upon me."

Did not Jesus say when you are converted – in other words, after you have dealt with this and found the personal victory – go and minister your victory to others, so they might also gain victory. The key to conversion is repentance. When Peter "wept bitterly" he was flooded with repentance and healing. And now a few years later Peter was able to put his finger on the motivation of the heart of Simon and minister to him the same forgiveness and healing that Peter had found.

Eph 4:31 *Let all bitterness, and wrath, and anger, and clamor, and evil speaking, be put away from you, with all malice:*

Hebrews 12:15 *Looking diligently lest any man fail of the grace of God; lest any root of bitterness springing up trouble [you], and thereby many be defiled;*

There are significant warnings about how bitterness must be dealt with and discarded so that the bitter person might find his freedom and hence enable him to minister to others freely and thereby not taint the Good News of Jesus Christ.

Gen 27:34 *And when Esau heard the words of his father, he cried with a great and exceeding bitter cry, and said unto his father, Bless me, [even] me also, O my father.*

When Esau wept bitterly he never found repentance – evidently his weeping was in anger not in repentance – notice the demand he makes through his tears. Esau is saying through his tears-bless me bless me – a true sign of anger not humility and repentance. Esau was not asking for a return of his birthright – this evidently meant nothing to him. He was pleading for the blessings only.

Whereas in the weeping of Peter no demands were made, he went off with his tail between his legs.

Bitterness is a place of defilement in the heart of a believer. The bitter person is focused on himself and what he is not getting. It is contrary to all the key words of the Kingdom that describe the character and motivations of believers.

Iniquity is that place in our soul where we have a tendency toward particular sin. It runs in families just like physical genetics. Things like heart disease, types of cancer, poor eyesight and on and on, run in families. Likewise habitual lying, stealing, cheating, and all the other types of sins run in families. Of course there are always exceptions to the rule and sometimes generations seem to skip certain things. An iniquity is at the root of sin. It is where sin is harbored in our heart and manifest as we give ourselves over to that tendency. It seems that every person is faced with dealing with their own generational iniquities.

It has been said that it takes 5 generations of not drinking to break the iniquity of alcoholism in a family. In other words there is a propensity to drink and when given into the possibility to become an alcoholic is ever present.

While we are at it – let's consider again the sin of homosexuality. Like ALL OTHER SIN, there is an iniquity or root cause born in the soul of each person. When the "tendency" toward homosexuality is in a person and recognized at even a young age- it does not mean they are "sentenced" to a life of homosexuality. No more than when hate is evidenced in the heart of a young child do caring parents give up and say "oh our child was born to be a murderer there is nothing we can do about it. " (Jesus said, "it says thou shall not kill, but I say whosoever hates his brother is a murderer!") Or if a young child lies obsessively do parents give in and say "oh, he was born that way there is nothing we can do about it."

Every family has its tendencies, the healthy thing to do is to be open about them, and not hide them (as is often the case), and openly deal with them via repentance and guarded practice of living free from the sin of the tendency.

Often a bitter person is one that regards all that happens as either too much – when it is bad – or too little when it is good. Often they will take it upon themselves to correct the situation, and their bitterness flavors every action they take. The birth of the church could not be lead by a bitter man. Peter for his own sake and for the sake of the church must find deliverance from bitterness.

WOW, if you think of it, it doesn't get dealt with until a little over fifty days before the birth of the church! But that weeping response through tears of humility enabled Peter to find his deliverance once and for all. We see no examples of bitterness or bravado or silly claims in Peter over the next 35 or so years of his life's ministry in the early church.

Discussion Chapter Eleven
Peter's Conversion
PART 2

1) What did Peter's denial uncover?

2) Why couldn't Jesus just tell Peter to quit it?

3) What is an iniquity?

4) What was the difference between Peter's tears and Esau's tears?

5) What does bitterness do to a person?

CHAPTER TWELVE
PETER'S DILEMMA AT
THE EMPTY TOMB

<u>Luke 24:12</u> *But Peter arose and ran to the tomb; and stooping down, he saw the linen cloths lying by themselves; and he departed, marveling to himself at what had happened.*

<u>John 20:1-9</u> *Now the first DAY of the week Mary Magdalene went to the tomb early, while it was still dark, and saw THAT the stone had been taken away from the tomb. Then she ran and came to Simon Peter, and to the other disciple, whom Jesus loved, and said to them, "They have taken away the Lord out of the tomb, and we do not know where they have laid Him." Peter therefore went out, and the other disciple, and were going to the tomb. So they both ran together, and the other disciple outran Peter and came to the tomb first.*

And he, stooping down and looking in, saw the linen cloths lying THERE; yet he did not go in. Then Simon Peter came, following him, and went into the tomb; and he saw the linen cloths lying THERE, and the handkerchief that had been around His head, not lying with the linen cloths, but folded together in a place by itself. Then the other disciple, who came to the tomb first, went in also; and he saw and believed. For as yet they did not know the Scripture, that He must rise again from the dead.

We must all learn from this example of Peter and his struggle at the grave site. We can look at this account in the Bible and say in our mind – "what a dummy, Jesus told him three times at least that He would die and rise again! Why is Peter standing there not knowing what is going on?"

To grasp "Spiritual truth" it takes "spiritual capacity." We are people with a soul, a spirit, and a body. Thus, there are three parts to us, which means there are three levels or dimensions that we live in. To better understand this, we can take a person who physically looks great, has great vital signs, great strength, but who is very sick. His body could be in great shape, but maybe his "soul" is sick – that place where his mind, will, and emotion reside – and he may still need to be hospitalized.

Notice that when Peter looked in at the grave clothes laying there without a body that he "wondered within him." Meaning that he could not get his mind around what he was seeing. He was not asking for "help from above," but rather he was trying to make "sense" of the scene by using his 5 senses to grasp the turn of events – Jesus died and was buried, but now where is the body?

In the world we pay a lot of attention to the soul and the body but we have very little understanding of the "spirit" part of the person. The "spirit" side of a person is harder to get a hold of, in terms of understanding. When a person is "born again" actually what is taking place is that the spirit of a person is brought back to life and now has the capacity to grasp spiritual truth and spiritual reality.

We think in terms of four dimensions – height – width – depth – and time. But scientists now tell us there are actually eleven dimensions. So there are seven we do not "see" or for that matter understand. We have already seen in scripture where Isaiah had the "curtain pulled back" and was allowed to see into the heavenly realm – or into another dimension. In the book of Acts we have this account of Stephen the first martyr of the church – where he was also allowed to see in the heavenly realm, or heavenly dimension.

Acts 7:55,56 *But he, being full of the Holy Spirit, gazed into heaven and saw the glory of God, and Jesus standing at the right hand of God, and said, "Look! I see the heavens opened and the Son of Man standing at the right hand of God!"*

Eyes to see spiritually come to us by way of us being filled with the Holy Spirit. When Peter came to the empty tomb he was not "filled with the Holy Ghost." He had for that matter not even been born again yet – and he was not able to grasp the "spiritual truth" of the resurrection. He was trying to process through natural interpretation and natural reasoning and it made no sense.

Notice the moment of salvation for the disciples:

John 20:19-22 *Then, the same day at evening, being the first DAY of the week, when the doors were shut where the disciples were assembled, for fear of the Jews, Jesus came and stood in the midst, and said to them, "Peace BE with you." When He had said this, He showed them HIS hands and His side. Then the disciples were glad when they saw the Lord. So Jesus said to them again, "Peace to you! As the Father has sent Me, I also send you." And when He had said this, He breathed on THEM, and said to them, "Receive the Holy Spirit.*

Jesus breathed on them the Holy Ghost and from then on they had the discernment to understand the spiritual dimension of the Kingdom of God on earth. They now had the **capacity** for spiritual things. Capacity and exercising ourselves in it are two different things. But at least now they could think of things spiritual, speak of things spiritual, and understand the spiritual dynamics of the Kingdom of God on earth.

This is how it works;

Rom 8:16 *The Spirit itself bears witness with our spirit, that we are the children of God:*

Let's look into this matter more closely, because in the western church there is very little understanding of the spiritual dynamics of what is going in the life of the church. Usually people interpret everything in church based on human rationale. The term political correctness is just that – political kingdom talking – and has nothing to do with the Kingdom of God and its moral correctness.

John 6:48-71 *I am the bread of life. Your fathers ate the manna in the wilderness, and are dead. This is the bread which comes down from heaven that one may eat of it and not die. I am the living bread which came down from heaven. If anyone eats of this bread, he will live forever; and the bread that I shall give is My flesh, which I shall give for the life of the world."*

The Jews therefore quarreled among themselves, saying, "How can this Man give us HIS flesh to eat?" Then Jesus said to them, "Most assuredly, I say to you, unless you eat the flesh of the Son of Man and drink His blood, you have no life in you. Whoever eats My flesh and drinks My blood has eternal life, and I will raise him up at the last day. For My flesh is food indeed, [fn8] and My blood is drink indeed. He who eats My flesh and drinks My blood abides in Me, and I in him. As the living Father sent Me, and I live because of the Father, so he who feeds on Me will live because of Me. This is the bread which came down from heaven—not as your fathers ate the manna, and are dead. He who eats this bread will live forever."

These things He said in the synagogue as He taught in Capernaum. Therefore many of His disciples, when they heard THIS, *said, "This is a hard saying; who can understand it?" When Jesus knew in Himself that His disciples complained about this, He said to them, "Does this offend you?* WHAT *then if you should see the Son of Man ascend where He was before? It is the Spirit who gives life; the flesh profits nothing. The words that I speak to you are spirit, and* THEY *are life. But there are some of you who do not believe." For Jesus knew from the beginning who they were who did not believe, and who would betray Him. And He said,*

"Therefore I have said to you that no one can come to Me unless it has been granted to him by My Father." From that TIME *many of His disciples went back and walked with Him no more. Then Jesus said to the twelve, "Do you also want to go away?" But Simon Peter answered Him, "Lord, to whom shall we go? You have the words of eternal life. Also we have come to believe and know that You are the Christ, the Son of the living God."*

Jesus answered them, "Did I not choose you, the twelve, and one of you is a devil?" He spoke of Judas Iscariot, THE SON *of*

Simon, for it was he who would betray Him, being one of the twelve.

This teaching is hard to understand and in many respects makes no "sense" at all. We would normally think that the goal is to get "everyone we can to join the group." But this is not the way of the Kingdom of God. The goal of the Kingdom is to get everyone to join with us that the Father has called. And then of those called only those who will come on His terms and not on some humanistic "feel good" terms will be eligible.

Above Jesus offers a teaching that the normal thinking person would say is so far out in its natural ramifications that this proves this "teacher" is too extreme and radical. His teachings are illogical and make no sense to a large segment of His followers. And many did leave.

But Jesus was saying words here that while to the natural mind were crazy, He was not speaking to the natural mind. He was speaking to the spiritual mind. The teaching was so obviously "out there" in scope that the people that were joining up for the wrong reasons were being put to the test. Many heard this teaching and decided to leave – this man Jesus was too radical – he crossed the line, so they bailed out. It sounds disgusting and pagan to speak of "eating flesh and blood."

But as we can recognize today Jesus was speaking of a future time, and He was speaking of a spiritual event that would take place at what we call the Lord's Supper in the church today.

There was another time when right after the feeding of the 5,000 that Jesus said this:

John 6:14,15 Then those men, when they had seen the sign that Jesus did, said, "This is truly the Prophet who is to come into the world." Therefore when Jesus perceived that they were about to come and take Him by force to make Him king, He departed again to the mountain by Himself alone.

Sure they wanted Him to be king – with a small k – because he could miraculously feed them! But no man makes Jesus king – He is King (with a capital K) because it is His place and purpose in our lives. These things are spiritually discerned.

When a local church is faced with issues – whether a building program, a missionary program, a children's program, a worship style, a preaching style, or who should be in leadership, or what the vision is for that church, or what activities should the church promote, or what curriculum should be followed in Sunday School, or any of the other matters that come to a church – we have a tendency to evaluate and decide based on human rationale and not in the "spirit." The question always is not only "what would God have us do, but how would God have us do it?"

The obvious is usually not the "spiritual way." So Peter swimming in questions at the grave is understandable in the context. To know and grasp the "ways of God" here on earth requires our new birth in the Kingdom of God, and requires our being filled with the Holy Spirit.

It has become a place of unnecessary controversy regarding being filled with the Spirit. There are those that say we are filled with the Spirit when we are born again – or come to the place of repentance and acknowledgement of our sins and our realization that only Jesus could pay for our sins. Then there are those that say we need a "second" experience of being Baptized in the Holy Spirit.

John the Baptist clearly taught that One that would follow him would baptize us in the Holy Spirit – and His name is Jesus. Rather than choke on a gnat, is it not reasonable to consider that there is more to God and more about God that we all want to spend daily time in apprehending and seeking with all our heart and soul? No person's experience with God should ever be minimized. But at the same time none of us has experienced all there is of God.

Peter's journey of faith proves to us, just as our own journey reveals to us that no matter what we know or experience in God there is more. For any of us to think we have all there is, or that we already have the Baptism of the Holy Spirit in the sense that we have all there is of it – is actually arrogant and religious.

Paul said he died daily- meaning to his own ways of thinking and doing things. As long as we are in this earthly suit, there are ebbs and flows of how we move in the Spirit of God. We need to actually be filled daily with the Holy Spirit. We need a fresh infilling and a constant infilling as we live in the constraints of this fleshly body.

There is a security we all can have in God that being filled with the Holy Spirit we will be able to anticipate the empty tomb and not be surprised by it. We will discern spiritual truth, spiritual direction, and be able to make spiritual decisions.

In fact, by being filled with the Holy Spirit of God we are enabled to worship God in spirit and truth – after all these are the kind of people God is looking for in the earth.

<u>John 4:23,24</u> *But the hour is coming, and now is, when the true worshipers will worship the Father in spirit and truth; for the Father is seeking such to worship Him. God IS Spirit, and those who worship Him must worship in spirit and truth."*

I read a bumper sticker the other day that said "religion requires leaving your mind at the door." So, after describing the importance of moving and thinking in the spirit realm what about the mind, what role does our intellect play in our faith?

Let me give a sentence that best sums up this dilemma for me easily. When the direction of the spirit seems contrary to the natural mind, and I obey and do it anyway, I find out after the fact that my mind now sees how and why it was the best thing to do. Obeying the Spirit is a little like hindsight; it is 20-20 vision before the fact rather than after the fact. Virtually every time I obey the Spirit I find after the fact my mind is able to catch up and realize that it was the best course of action to take although my mind could not grasp it before the fact.

One of the functions of the Holy Spirit is that He will guide us into all truth. When I read scripture and rely on the Holy Spirit interacting with my spirit, my mind gets involved and learns how to process spiritual truth in my mind. Our mind and intellect are a wonder, with far greater capacity than most of us come near to using. Our minds can be trained to "think" spiritually. Contrary to the bumper sticker above – our minds cannot be left at the door. We are commanded to use our minds to think on things above and not think on things below. We can learn to think about heavenly things that the average person not filled with the Holy Spirit has no idea exists.

In the local church, a problem comes into play in that if it seems like everything is riding on the spiritual leader(s) and the people have no say - then the fear of the people is that the church is vulnerable to manipulation and control. But this is where it is everyone's own responsibility to test the spirits – to know whether they be of God or not.

Acts 17:11 *These were more fair-minded than those in Thessalonica, in that they received the word with all readiness, and searched the Scriptures daily to find out whether these things were so.*

So as Peter learned after being saved and filled with the Holy Spirit all the things he had been taught by Jesus now made sense. In fact his mind was enriched and wisdom gained was evident as the leaders of the synagogue noticed when he argued before the court.

Acts 4:13 *Now when they saw the boldness of Peter and John, and perceived that they were uneducated and untrained men, they marveled. And they realized that they had been with Jesus.*

This proves the point that our minds can catch up and wisdom gained as we walk in the fullness of God's Spirit on a daily basis. We are admonished to think on those things above. Our issue is we get preoccupied by the things below – meaning the things that interact with the five senses. There is another level of thinking and living. It has been said that "so and so" is so heavenly minded he is no earthly good. But as time has gone on I have come to take issue with this quip. There is a place where the things of this earth do grow faintly dim. It is more important to grasp the spiritual side of life.

Outline Chapter Twelve
Peter's Dilemma at the Empty Tomb

1) Describe what you think was going through Peter's mind at the empty tomb.

2) What was the solution to enable Peter and all the disciples to understand what was going on?

3) How would you describe what it means to be filled with the Spirit?

4) What role does our mind play in our faith?

5) How can a local church come to terms with the leading and direction of the Holy Spirit?

CHAPTER THIRTEEN
TRYING TO MAKE SENSE
OF IT ALL PART 1

<u>John 21:1-7</u> *After these things Jesus showed Himself again to the disciples at the Sea of Tiberias, and in this way He showed HIMSELF: Simon Peter, Thomas called the Twin, Nathanael of Cana in Galilee, the* SONS *of Zebedee, and two others of His disciples were together. Simon Peter said to them, "I am going fishing."They said to him, "We are going with you also." They went out and immediately got into the boat, and that night they caught nothing.*

But when the morning had now come, Jesus stood on the shore; yet the disciples did not know that it was Jesus. Then Jesus said to them, "Children, have you any food?"They answered Him, "No."And He said to them, "Cast the net on the right side of the boat, and you will find SOME.*" So they cast, and now they were not able to draw it in because of the multitude of fish. Therefore that disciple whom Jesus loved said to Peter, "It is the Lord!" Now when Simon Peter heard that it was the Lord, he put on* HIS *outer garment (for he had removed it), and plunged into the sea.*

Things weren't coming together for the disciples. Even though they had the Holy Spirit in the dimension of a born again experience – that is their spirit was alive and available to the spiritual realm – they had no sense of direction at this time.

They had seen Jesus a couple of times, and He spoke of lofty things, and yes, He did rise from the dead, but now what? They had not been given specific instructions for how to get this "church thing started." They were still trying to figure out is He going to go to Rome and take over now? Is He going to set up His Kingdom in Jerusalem? When is He going to get this Kingdom thing going?

Often, shortly after the grand impact of salvation and filling with the Spirit there comes the thought now what? And of course, on the human level without clear direction we go back to that which we know and can take comfort in. So when Peter says here "I go a fishing" in the Greek, the sense of the expression is this; well, I guess I will go back to my vocation and work full time in catching fish. Others with him agreed and somehow they found a boat and cast off and started fishing.

Human reasoning and human frustration can get in the way of coming to grips with spiritual reality. They had not learned to wait – most of us haven't – and felt like they had to go on with life. Well, they fished all night and the nets were empty – sound familiar? Isn't this how it all started?

A voice called out on their return to shore asking had they caught anything? They were told to cast on the "right side" of the ship and low and behold the nets were full. The disciple John said that it is the Lord who called out and told us to fish the other side – and as only Peter could do – he threw on a coat and jumped in and swam ashore to see Jesus.

Spiritual life can be very frustrating when measured in natural terms. But in the Kingdom the timing of God is His means of rounding off the edges. In addition, the waiting period or the in between time will build a demand in the heart of a believer that will pull on the call of God so that the call is taken seriously and followed.

We have got to see and hear the relief in the heart and mind of Peter here. Trapped in frustration of no fish after all night trying, and trapped in the frustration of not knowing what to do next, Peter leaped again into the anointing of the Lord and came a swimming to the shore. We have to realize that when Jesus had left them the last time they legitimately wondered if they would ever see Him again.

We must realize here that things were happening very quickly. I can tell you I wish that from salvation to getting filled with the Spirit and my launch into ministry could have taken place in 50 days! But thank God in my case it didn't because I had much to deal with in my own heart. It is not so much the length of time here for us to note but the process.

There is a heart preparation required in the hearts of all new believers prior to and during finding the call of God on our lives. I see here that Peter and those with him did not know what to do next. So they went to what they did know to do, and the Lord showed them that the rewards from fishing were so uncertain. Then again the authority Jesus had over fish proved once more to verify His role in their lives. It's almost here like Jesus wanted to stamp out the temptation for the disciples to ever again return to their former lives. And He did in fact for it was never again a consideration – regardless of the ups and downs of their life in ministry.

TRYING TO MAKE SENSE OF IT ALL –PART 2

<u>John 21:8-22</u> *But the other disciples came in the little boat (for they were not far from land, but about two hundred cubits), dragging the net with fish. Then, as soon as they had come to land, they saw a fire of coals there, and fish laid on it, and bread.*

Jesus said to them, "Bring some of the fish which you have just caught." Simon Peter went up and dragged the net to land, full of large fish, one hundred and fifty-three; and although there were so many, the net was not broken. Jesus said to them, "Come AND *eat breakfast." Yet none of the disciples dared ask Him, "Who are You?"—knowing that it was the Lord. Jesus then came and took the bread and gave it to them, and likewise the fish.*

This IS *now the third time Jesus showed Himself to His disciples after He was raised from the dead.*

So when they had eaten breakfast, Jesus said to Simon Peter, "Simon, SON *of Jonah, do you love Me more than these?" He said to Him, "Yes, Lord; You know that I love You." He said to him, "Feed My lambs." He said to him again a second time, "Simon,* SON *of Jonah, do you love Me?" He said to Him, "Yes, Lord; You know that I love You." He said to him, "Tend My sheep." He said to him the third time, "Simon,* SON *of Jonah, do you love Me?" Peter was grieved because He said to him the third time, "Do you love Me?"And he said to Him, "Lord, You know all things; You know that I love You."Jesus said to him, "Feed My sheep.*

Most assuredly, I say to you, when you were younger, you girded yourself and walked where you wished; but when you are old, you will stretch out your hands, and another will gird you and carry YOU *where you do not wish." This He spoke, signifying by what death he would glorify God. And when He had spoken this, He said to him, "Follow Me." Then Peter, turning around, saw the disciple whom Jesus loved following, who also had leaned on His breast at the supper, and said, "Lord, who is the one who betrays You?" Peter, seeing him, said to Jesus, "But Lord, what* ABOUT *this man?" Jesus said to him, "If I will that he remain till I come, what* IS THAT *to you? You follow Me."*

Jesus needed to tap into a primal force within humanity. The reason for these eleven men to start this journey would have to be most compelling and would have to be strong enough to keep them going regardless of the barriers they would face along life's way.

I have had the privilege of meeting several great men and women who have been successful in building their business from the ground up. Not one of them did it for monetary gain! They each did it because they had an idea that they believed in and they wanted to perform the service or deliver the product that they dreamed about.

One day a visitor came to my office. The receptionist called and said Dave Thomas the founder of Wendy's was in the lobby and he wanted to meet me. So I went down and escorted him to my office and we sat and talked for about two hours. He wanted to hear my story – and I was able to share my faith as well as my business journey. He told me his story and I found it amazing. He worked for Colonel Sanders of KFC. He was mentored by him and after working with him for several years Dave had a vision of serving a "fresh hamburger." He dreamed how to do it and put all the plans and processes in place to get going. A common man and caring man became a multi-millionaire as a result of dreaming about delivering a fresh hamburger. The financial rewards were the result of the dream not the goal of the dream.

We see Jesus calling on Peter and in reality calling them all, to grasp the significance of what He was appointing them to do in the Kingdom. The call was not based on personal gain for those called. Jesus does not offer positions with promises of fame and fortune. The call on Peter's life and the call on the lives of the disciples – and for that matter the call on all believers throughout the church age are based on the fundamental force of the universe- which is love. Jesus says, "Do you love me more than these?" These in this case meant the vocation of fishing. "These" can mean anything that we might love more than Him? Jesus is calling us all to His love. This is our dream – how can I love Jesus and show it?

Let's pause and start over and put yourself in the moment. Everything is calm around the charcoal fire – same kind of fire that Peter was around when he had denied Christ the third time!

They were all hungry and the fish was frying. They were relaxed and waiting.

Jesus says to Simon Peter do you love me more than these? Agape love – God's kind of love – and Peter answers I Phileo love you – brotherly love, fond of you kind of love. Feed my lambs. All is quiet at the fire. Jesus speaks up the second time and says to Simon son of Jonas do you Agape kind of love me Peter? No one else is saying a word. Peter answers and says, "I Phileo love you." Jesus says, "Feed my sheep." I sense a pause here with no Biblical authority to verify it. But we see something is deep at work here and this can lead us to envision a quiet powerful moment – a life changing moment, in the life of Peter and those with him.

My sense is that everything remains quiet, with the fire crackling, and the power of the moment weighing in on the participants. Jesus (perhaps quietly) says the third time to Simon son of Jonas, but with a different word for love – "Do you Phileo me?" Peter was grieved with this third question. I can sense in the spirit Peter's reminder of the agony he felt at the "other" charcoal fire. And just as he had denied Christ 3 times he now proclaimed with all his heart the third time, "Yea Lord thou knowest all things; thou knowest that I Phileo love thee." Jesus said feed my sheep.

The evidence in the life lived out by Peter is that this moment brought a complete healing in his heart. From this moment forward Peter never again looked back. He never again wondered what he should do or where he should go. There never again was ambivalence in action or thought. Jesus had touched that place in Peter that settled life's issues for Peter and the rest of the disciples. Love conquers all.

Do you love me and the demands I will put on you more than you love fishing? After thirteen years of full time ministry the biggest shock I had overall in the ministry was in seeing how few laborers there are available for the harvest. The vast majority is so busy and has so many other things ahead of their love of Jesus. Jesus said where your treasure is there is your heart also.

The Bible says I love God because He first loved me. In order for us to love God we must understand His love for us first. The test of the call was not I will do this for you if you will do that for me. That is how you get jobs in the world. The test was simply do you love me – more than these?

By the third time Jesus asked the question, Peter was becoming grieved in his heart. It was dawning on him that love and not gain was the fuel of the Kingdom here on earth. Truly he knew that Jesus loved him and truly he loved Jesus. The challenge by Jesus was based on the fact that if you do truly love me, then you will feed my sheep. The evidence of your love will be in the feeding of my sheep. If we go back to Peter's first encounter fishing with Jesus, there Jesus said "I will make you fishers of men!"

Please understand here that Jesus is taking a fisherman and asking him to be a farmer in the Kingdom. In all likelihood Peter knew very little about feeding lambs and sheep. But remember this is a "spiritual appeal" not a natural appeal. The bread to feed lambs and sheep was the bread of life not the fodder of the field. As Jesus had quoted Moses, man shall not live by bread alone, but by every word that proceeds from the Father.

Peter will you preach to the "lambs and sheep" of this world in my Name and teach them the ways of the Kingdom? The fuel that drives and motivates the workers in the church of Jesus Christ is love. Jesus was not appealing to Peter to be the head of the church. He was not offering Peter a title. He was bringing the relationship between Jesus and Peter to its core. Do you love me? This love connection is the basis for all Christian service. Love is eternal – meaning it does not die.

We are not called to serve because the people need us – we are called to serve because we love Him as He first loved us. We serve at His whim. When He calls us to a people, He will give us His love for those people as a burden in our own hearts. This love for the people group we serve will be the manifestation of our love for Him. We don't serve people for competitive gain or advantage over others. We serve out of love for Him. All other motives are wrong motives and will be revealed sooner or later.

There is one other point to be made from this passage. Jesus was prophesying that Peter would die as a result of this call. Jesus told him in older age they would take him to die and Peter would have no power to change that. As history bore out, Peter was sentenced to die by crucifixion and he pleaded that he was unworthy to die the same way his Messiah had died. He pleaded and was granted to die on the cross upside down. His love for Jesus was proven beyond a shadow of doubt and even in his dying breath!

It is vital to see that Jesus did not explain how this feeding process would work. He did not explain how the Church would get started. Jesus did not lay out an organization chart with positions defined and geography laid out.

What Jesus did lay out was the motive of the heart required before the first step could take place.

There is something that needs to be thought about at this point. Why did not Jesus just spell things out here on the shore? Why not just tell them what was going to happen and what they should do next? Perhaps the chief reason was that they were not ready. They still needed to be "filled with the Holy Spirit." And that was not going to take place until after Jesus left the earth. And in fact, it was not going to happen until they were willing to pray and seek the Lord for ten days after the ascension of Jesus.

The will of God for our lives always has conditions. There is likewise usually a confluence of events that need to come together so that the will of God unfolds before us. We can look back in our own lives and usually say if I had known all the steps I had to take before I took them I would perhaps not have wanted to take some of them and would have missed out on being where I am today in the Lord.

Jesus had said that He had to leave the earth so that "Another" like Him would come. This evidently meant that Jesus must physically leave the earth before the manifest Presence of the Holy Spirit and His work on earth could get started. We can take comfort in the Promises of Jesus. He said He would never leave us nor forsake us. He said He would work with us and confirm the Word of God with signs and wonders following.

As we come to the close of the life that Peter found while walking with Jesus during the ministry of Jesus on earth, we can clearly see the manifested change that took place. Peter was at all times a willing participant. He was quick to question what he had trouble understanding. He always was on the alert for what was next. As time went on we can see that Peter maintained his integrity. What he struggled with was an honest struggle. But let us be sure that Peter matured greatly in these 3 ½ years of walking with Jesus. Without forward planning and direction, Peter was left to recognize the "anointing" and go with it as we can see starting in Acts 2. He was to become the first to do the most dramatic things that the church would do as it was birthed.

But the fact remains that Peter found life – true life – which is eternal through his Savior who died and rose again from the dead - Jesus Christ. Every human being born has physical life but that life can be short lived. Without accepting the provision of eternal life through Jesus that life outside of Christ after physical death next brings spiritual "death" that means eternal separation from God.

May all who seek life find that same life in Christ Jesus!

Discussion Chapter Thirteen
Trying to Make Sense of it All
Parts 1 and 2

1) Why did Peter and the others decide to "go a fishing?"

2) Why do you think they caught no fish at first?

3) Why did Peter jump in the water to swim ashore?

4) Why did Jesus ask Peter 3 times if Peter loved Him?

5) Why didn't Jesus just spell things out so they would know what was coming next?

Made in the USA
Charleston, SC
27 April 2012